CARLOAD RITCHIE

CARLOAD RITCHIE

The Life and Times of
Harold F. Ritchie, World's
Greatest Salesman

[signed] Don Gillmor

DON GILLMOR

SUTHERLAND HOUSE
TORONTO, 2022

Sutherland House
416 Moore Ave., Suite 205
Toronto, ON M4G 1C9

Copyright © 2022 by Don Gillmor

All rights reserved, including the right to reproduce this book or portions thereof in any form whatsoever. For information on rights and permissions or to request a special discount for bulk purchases, please contact Sutherland House at info@sutherlandhousebooks.com

Sutherland House and logo are registered trademarks of The Sutherland House Inc.

First edition, August 2022

If you are interested in inviting one of our authors to a live event or media appearance, please contact sranasinghe@sutherlandhousebooks.com and visit our website at sutherlandhousebooks.com for more information about our authors and their schedules.

Manufactured in China
Cover designed by Lena Yang
Book composed by Karl Hunt

Library and Archives Canada Cataloguing in Publication
Title: Carload Ritchie : the life and times of Harold F. Ritchie, world's greatest salesman / Don Gillmor.
Other titles: Life and times of Harold F. Ritchie, world's greatest salesman
Names: Gillmor, Don, author.
Identifiers: Canadiana 20220176094 | ISBN 9781989555675 (hardcover)
Subjects: LCSH: Ritchie, Harold F., -1933 | LCSH: Businesspeople—Canada—Biography. | LCSH: Pharmaceutical industry—Canada—History. | LCGFT: Biographies.
Classification: LCC HD9665.5 .G55 2022 | DDC 338.4/76151092—dc23

ISBN 978-1-989555-67-5

Table of Contents

Prologue — vii

CHAPTER ONE: Manitoulin — 1

CHAPTER TWO: Alice Alberta — 23

CHAPTER THREE: The Travelling Salesman — 33

CHAPTER FOUR: From Selling to Buying — 53

CHAPTER FIVE: A Thing of Beauty — 77

CHAPTER SIX: Woodlands — 95

CHAPTER SEVEN: Carload's Legacy — 101

Sources — 119

Acknowledgments — 123

Prologue

HAROLD FRANKLIN RITCHIE died in 1933 of cardiac and respiratory failure during gall bladder surgery at Toronto General Hospital. He was fifty-two. "Death comes for the salesman," was the headline on *Time* magazine's obituary: "Last week, Death came to a squeaky-voiced Canadian named Harold F. Ritchie as he lay on a Toronto operating table. His name is not found on many rosters of the business great, yet he had good claim to the proud title of World's Greatest Salesman and his nom de guerre, immortal in the annals of super-salesmanship, was Carload Ritchie." His funeral was a private affair at his house, yet hundreds of business leaders and prominent politicians came to mourn him.

Carload Ritchie was one of Canada's richest men, and owner of the largest sales agency in the world. He operated in "every civilized country in the world except Russia" and travelled more than 200,000 kilometres a year, leaving him home for less than three months a year. When he was home, he was either at his elegant office on McCaul Street, or his Forest Hill mansion, or at his country estate, "Woodlands," on Lake Simcoe. Woodlands was set on seventy acres and featured seventeen-bedrooms and tennis courts. It had its own putting green, although Ritchie rarely golfed. In fact, he rarely walked or took any form of exercise.

Medium height and chubby, Carload Ritchie was not a physically prepossessing man. He smoked cigars, didn't drink, played the piano before going to bed, travelled with his own pillow, and possessed an extraordinary memory. Musically, his tastes ran to "sentimental gypsy music and Viennese waltzes, which he would listen to with tears running down his plump cheeks," according to *Time*. But his companies, among them Harold F. Ritchie Co. and International Proprietaries Co. Ltd, were more profitable than most of Canada's banks.

He wasn't part of the Toronto establishment, for several reasons: he was rarely around; he was a salesman; and it didn't help that he was provincial (born in Bobcaygeon, Ontario, and raised in Little Current on Manitoulin Island). In the eyes of the city's corporate elite, he was an outsider, a peripatetic Presbyterian when the Methodists ran Toronto. And he lived in Forest Hill Village, not yet part of Toronto, isolated from the city's elite, many of whom were in mansions on Sherbourne and Jarvis streets. In any event, he wasn't much interested in being part

PROLOGUE

of the establishment. His life was sales. He could stay up until 4:00 a.m. talking to buyers or his salesmen. He would forget to eat when caught up in a sales trip, and then he would eat too much. Selling was his greatest passion, one of his few passions outside of his family. He also loved fast cars, fast boats, and fast airplanes, but mostly because they got him to his next appointment quickly.

After his death, the *Mail and Empire* newspaper wrote, "He was known more widely in London and New York than he was in Toronto. His name appeared often in commercial circles, but he was seldom prominent in Toronto otherwise. Beside his office and his home, very little else held much interest for him." He avoided publicity. "He didn't like his own name in interviews," another obituary pointed out. "He turned reporters to his close friend and director, Sid Screaton, or told reporters to write the story and 'leave me out.'" In one of the few in-depth interviews he gave, less than three years before his death, a journalist noted, "Mr. Ritchie consented to break his lifelong habit about no publicity." The most comprehensive profiles of him may have been his obituaries, which appeared in dozens of newspapers. Although heralded as the greatest salesman in the world, and one of Canada's richest men, he was an enigma to most Canadians.

In North America, it was the golden age of sales. In 2005, Walter Friedman, a professor at the Harvard Business School, wrote a book titled *Birth of a Salesman: The Transformation of Selling in America*, where he argued that the birth of modern salesmanship occurred in the late-nineteenth and early twentieth century. Dale Carnegie's classic *How to Win Friends and Influence People* would be published in 1937, touting the lessons the author had learned in the trade. Carnegie turned these lessons into a distinctly American philosophy based on optimism, confidence, and perseverance. "Most of the important things in the world have been accomplished by people who have kept on trying when there seemed to be no hope at all," he said. *How to Win Friends and Influence People* would become a cultural touchstone, and sales were becoming a new religion, the most identifiable part of North American business. Harold Ritchie, embodying all of Carnegie's qualities, was poised somewhere between the religion's most devout disciple and its messiah.

What did he sell? His first product lines were staples that everyone needed: tea, coffee, rice, flour. But as his empire grew, he branched out into something else people needed: to feel better. The demand for patent medicines, over-the-counter nostrums that cured all ills, had been growing in the last half of the nineteenth century. Harold saw them advertised in the Manitoulin newspaper when he was a child. They had names like "Buffalo Lithia Water" and "ABC Liniment" (named for its three primary ingredients: aconite, belladonna, and chloroform). If it was medicinal, the potion often had a doctor's name in the title: "Dr. Bateman's Pectoral Drops," or "Dr. Thomas' Eclectric Oil," which touted the healing power of electricity. If it was for infants or children, it

PROLOGUE

often contained a woman's name. For instance, "Mrs. Winslow's Soothing Syrup" did, in fact, soothe crying babies, relying on morphine for its results. These medicines ranged from innocuous to effective to fraudulent. They claimed to cure everything from indigestion to cholera to distemper to "female complaints." Ritchie avoided the fraudulent and toxic products, and several of the products he sold and later owned, like Eno's Fruit Salts and Bovril, are still sold a century later. He understood the western world's increasing interest in health (despite his carelessness about his own health) and anticipated the drug revolution.

"There is reason to believe that Carload Ritchie died on the threshold of a vaster career," said *Time* magazine. That vaster career may well have been a pharmaceutical empire.

CHAPTER ONE

Manitoulin

THE RITCHIE FAMILY WERE lowland Scots, but by the eighteenth century, like many Presbyterian Scots, they had immigrated to Northern Ireland, settling in County Tyrone. From there, James Ritchie and his wife, Elizabeth, lit out for the United States in 1833, part of a steady flow of Irish immigrants. Between 1815 and 1845, one million people left the Emerald Isle. Prospects at home were limited, and word coming from earlier immigrants to Canada and the US told of better opportunities. The Ritchies sailed to America with plans to migrate to Upper Canada, but James became severely ill on the ship. While waiting for him to recover, the couple found land and began farming in the Madrid/Waddington area of New York State.

CARLOAD RITCHIE

In 1855, their son John, who had come over with his parents from Ireland as a boy, decided he would be the one to reach the family's original destination. He was married to Mary McCullough and they had three children. Mary was pregnant with their fourth and on her way north when she gave birth in Ogdensburg, New York, on the Canadian border (later the site of a clandestine 1940 meeting between Canadian Prime Minister Mackenzie King and US president Franklin Roosevelt to sign a continental defence pact). William David Ritchie, Harold's father, was born on US soil, but the family quickly crossed into Canada.

The young Ritchies ended up in Bobcaygeon, a village of fewer than 1,000 people in the Kawartha Lakes area of Ontario. John ran a hotel. His father, James, ended up in Bobcaygeon, as well, after the death of his wife in New York State.

Young William grew up in Bobcaygeon and worked as a mechanic and mill hand. He married Matilda Jane Johnston in 1876, and they had a daughter, Mary Lavinia, two years later. Harold was born three years after that, on February 20, 1881. When he was seven, his family moved to the village of Little Current on Manitoulin Island. Little Current was smaller than Bobcaygeon and very remote. It may have been an offer of employment that drew William there. His first job on the island was as shipper and inspector at the Red Mill in Little Current.

MANITOULIN

It would have been a leap of faith to move to Manitoulin in 1888. The island was cold, remote, and with little in the way of civilizing infrastructure. Canada, itself, was still in its infancy. A tipsy John A. Macdonald was still prime minister. Louis Riel had been hanged only three years earlier. Alberta wasn't yet a province. The Ritchies were moving into a largely unpopulated wilderness.

The Indigenous people had been on Manitoulin Island for 9,500 years. The name Manitoulin means "Spirit Island," home of the Great Spirit or "Kitche Manitou." In the mythology of Algonquian-speaking peoples, it was Kitche Manitou who created the universe. He made mankind last and bestowed upon it his greatest gift, the power to dream. Most of the Indigenous people on the island are descended from the Ojibwe; these include the Ojibwe from Lake Superior, the Mississauga of the Mississauga River and Manitoulin; the Odawa of Georgian Bay; and the Potawatami of the west side of Lake Huron.

The first European on Manitoulin was the French Jesuit priest, Joseph Poncet, who arrived in 1648 to establish a mission. It was short-lived. Having formed an alliance with the French, the Indigenous nations in the southern part of Georgian Bay were among the first to be decimated by European diseases, losing roughly half their population by the mid-seventeenth century. The Iroquois Confederacy took advantage of this and expanded the raids against their traditional rivals. The raids extended to other tribes living on Manitoulin, and in 1650, Poncet gave up the mission there and retreated to Quebec. Many of the Indigenous people left with him, some going to Île d'Orleans. The Odawa were the last to remain on Manitoulin, but by 1652 they had been driven off the island by the Iroquois as well.

To eradicate the European diseases, Manitoulin was set on fire by Indigenous people. It was essentially uninhabited for more than a century, waiting for the vegetation and wildlife to finally return. It wasn't until 1833 that the Roman Catholic Church set up a permanent mission at Little Current, which was called Wewebijiwang by the Anishinaabe residents. The 1860 Little Current census shows a population of fifty-two people, mostly Indigenous families. They grew corn, potatoes, peas, and beans, and raised horses, cows, pigs, oxen, and chickens. They fished and harvested maple syrup and sold wood and supplies to the steamships on Lake Huron.

In 1862, a treaty was offered to the roughly 1,300 Indigenous residents. Not everyone could read, and so they weren't aware that part of the treaty stipulated that they would be relocated, and that they couldn't remain on potential harbours, town sites, or sawmill sites. Little Current represented all three. Fewer than half the existing Indigenous population agreed to the treaty, yet most of the island was taken by the Crown. The result of this inequity was an unresolved feud between the government and Indigenous residents; the Wikwemikong Peninsula remains one of only two unceded territories in the province.

By 1864, there were seventy-nine people in Little Current, including non-Indigenous families that had moved there in the wake of the treaty. Two years later, land on Manitoulin was officially put up for sale by the government, costing fifty cents an acre, with a maximum of 200 acres. There weren't many takers and in the following year the price dropped to twenty cents an acre, with a maximum of 400 acres.

By 1868 a few more settlers had arrived, and there was a store and a tavern. In 1870, there were "about five or six white families in the village," according to an account by T. J. Patten, a resident. It grew quickly with the promise of cheap land, and by 1880 two licensed hotels had opened. There was a booming tourist trade and people came by steamship for the fishing and hunting (deer, ducks, partridge or ruffed grouse, and the now-extinct passenger pigeon). The dramatic scenery was also a draw: quartzite and limestone ridges, as well as stretches of the Canadian Shield dotted with evergreens and stands of poplar and birch.

When the Ritchies arrived in Little Current in 1888, a typhoid epidemic was raging. The local two-room school closed for a month. By early November, eight children were dead, and more died of measles before the year was over. The town's undertaker was also a furniture maker; he made more coffins than furniture that year.

A third hotel was built in 1888 and, according to a resident at the time, "there was considerable drunken and disorderly conduct."

CARLOAD RITCHIE

The Expositor announced that "the streets are getting so that no respectable woman will venture out after dark." It was a wild town, essentially a frontier town. A court house was built in 1890 to deal with the lawless. To balance all the sin, redemption was at hand in the form of three churches: Methodist, Presbyterian, and Anglican. Roman Catholic and United churches eventually followed (all but the Anglican Church burned down over the years, the United Church more than once, and the Methodist Church several times).

Little Current had a few hundred residents and a stream of shipping traffic: freighters, tugs, steamboats, passenger ships. The Red Mill had opened in 1886 after moving from Barrie, and the island would soon become a major lumber centre. Immediately after the Ritchies arrived, the Mansion House Hotel (now the Anchor Inn) was built on the harbour. A hotel in nearby Gore Bay was built two years later, with room for 100 guests to accommodate the growing tourist trade. Whatever the reason for William and Matilda to move there, it proved to be a good decision. Little Current was thriving, mostly because of all the boat traffic. It may have been isolated, but it was also a hub, supplying fuel for steamships, shipping lumber, and accommodating tourists. William soon left the sawmill and opened a bakery and a confectionary. The bakery was soon doing a booming business. At its height, it produced 700 loaves of bread daily, supplying not only the town but the tugboats that frequented the port. William added groceries and provisions to his store on Robinson Street. The family lived above the store and both Harold and his sister helped out (Harold's brother William Morland wasn't born until 1894, thirteen years younger).

Ritchie's Store faced onto the harbour, and steamboat whistles were the soundtrack of Harold's childhood. When the steamboat whistle blew in Little Current, the whole town stopped and rushed to the docks. In the early days, the schoolteacher, Tom Reid, dismissed school when he heard the whistle, regardless of the time of day, and rushed to the docks to tend bar. Churches emptied out in mid-benediction. The boats were the lifeblood of the town.

Ritchie's store had two competitors, Sim's and Turner's, and all three regularly placed ads in the local paper. Early on, the stores essentially issued their own money as there wasn't a bank in town. Cheques would circulate as a form of currency, and the store owners sometimes bartered with farmers for produce. Banks were wary of transporting cash over Lake Huron in winter; teams of horses had been known to plunge through the ice. It wasn't until the lumber mills became prosperous that the banks were willing to take the chance, and the Merchant Bank of Canada (later purchased by the Bank of Montreal) set up the first branch on the island.

The Expositor newspaper had been established in Manitowaning in 1879, and moved to Little Current in 1888. It served the island

and, depending on ownership, veered between a vitriolic Liberal paper and a vitriolic Conservative paper. It consisted mostly of international news and human-interest stories lifted from other papers. Local news was contained in a few columns titled Local & Personal, and featured one or two lines on the state of the island's citizens: "Mr. R.D. Fleming is confined to the house with la grippe;" "The mental condition of Mr. Kruger is causing serious apprehension." Death notices tended to be economical: "Mr. Joseph Sant of Clarksburg was killed Saturday by his team running away." No story was too mundane to merit a line in the personal section: "W. H. Williams spent Sunday with his family;" "John Conan accidentally fell off his ladder while putting up the storm windows on his house." The death notices were leavened with syndicated features: "Are Widows Going Out of Fashion?"; "About Tiresome Women"; "When Does a Woman Grow Old?". Ads for Stanfield's unshrinkable underwear and cures for Dropsy would appear amid the personals in the same font, blurring the distinction between advertising and news, something that would become much more pronounced 150 years later.

One thing that remains constant throughout the early decades of the *Expositor* are ads for patent medicines. Burdock Blood Bitters, which was regularly featured, cured a variety of ills, including biliousness, dyspepsia, jaundice, dropsy, disordered liver, and culminating, finally, in a "Permanent Cure for Cancer." Dodd's Kidney Pills, Milburn's Heart and Nerve Pills for Weak People;

Winters Instant Cough Cure; and the Voltaic Belt for Nervous Debilitated Men were all seen repeatedly in the newspaper. Ads for Scott's Emulsion, a company Harold would eventually own, also appeared regularly.

Little Current was incorporated as a town in 1890, and William Ritchie served on the first city council and the school board. He was also active in the Presbyterian church and became a Mason after a lodge was established. There were three sawmills by then, and Little Current was one of the biggest mill towns on Lake Huron. In 1892, a telegraph line was established, and Manitoulin was connected to the larger world.

For Harold, summers offered a bucolic life of fishing and swimming. In 1890 the town formed a baseball team called the Little Current Unknowns. Unfortunately, the league was also unknown, and it wasn't clear that they actually played anyone. Winter brought a 300-metre toboggan slide, and a skating rink. A hockey team was eventually organized and games with neighbouring Gore Bay were notable for their violence. These weren't the only sports. There was horse racing, although initially it was seasonal, taking place on the ice. In 1898, a dirt track was built for summer racing. Notwithstanding these diversions, and the new-fangled telegraph, Harold's upbringing was isolated. The mainland was a long boat ride away in summer, a lengthy, perilous drive over the ice in winter. It wasn't easy getting around the island, either, so his world was largely contained in Little Current.

CARLOAD RITCHIE

Harold's first teacher would likely have been Miss Dawson. But she had seventy-nine students and a measles outbreak to deal with, and left after her first year. Later, the town was able to expand the school and hire more teachers. In the 1890 local election, W.D. Ritchie's business competitor, T.C. Sims, was declared mayor, while Ritchie and his other competitor, B.H. Turner, were elected to council.

Harold helped out at the store and listened to the salesmen when they came by, two or three times a year. To a ten-year-old boy, they seemed glamorous figures: travelling the country, talking to people, telling their stories. They represented adventure and the outside world. Ritchie noted that one salesman would be selling vinegar, another pickles, another spices, and another tea and coffee. He asked why one salesman didn't represent more products, given the difficulty and expense of travel. He was told that this was "the coming thing."

American businessmen came to Manitoulin Island to fish, and for a fee, the teenaged Ritchie would row them to where the fish were biting. He used these moments to bounce his sales ideas off the visitors, and to ask them about their own businesses. By the time he was twelve, he understood that salesmen were paid a five percent commission on what they sold, and that they were going about it all wrong.

In his last year of school, Harold realized he would need good grades in order to accomplish all he wanted. He wasn't sure how he was going to fare on the final exams, so he climbed through the window of the schoolhouse and copied down the exam questions. In the spirit of solidarity, he shared the questions with his schoolmates. To the teacher's surprise, despite uneven results throughout the school year, everyone rose to the occasion and passed the final exams.

Small towns are often knit together by intermarriage and shared tragedy. Manitoulin was isolated and the climate was harsh so it had its share of both. Robert Boyter was the Keeper of the Janet Head Lighthouse on Gore Bay, and in March 1885, his wife Isabella and son David left Janet Head to cross the ice to the town of Spanish on the mainland. They were in a sleigh pulled by oxen. The snow was heavy and turning to slush in the first glimpse of spring and the oxen moved so slowly they were forced to stop and spend the night on Darch Island, halfway across. It was a bitter night, and they were both freezing. The next day they made it to the mainland but Isabella died a few days later. David's feet were frostbitten and both had to be amputated.

Robert Boyter got news of this tragedy—his wife dead, his son in dire straits—and hired George Thorne and his team of horses to take him across the bay. With them was another man and two young girls, eleven-year-old Mary Baxter and Nellie O'Shea. Partway across the ice they were caught in a blizzard. An ice trail was marked but they couldn't see it through the driving snow. They were finally forced to stop and spend the night on the ice. In the morning, the horses refused to move, and George Thorne set off on foot, walking to the mainland. Hours later, a rescue party arrived, but by that time Mary Baxter was dead. Nellie O'Shea needed to have part of her frostbitten foot amputated.

Robert was blamed for the death of Mary Baxter. There were court cases, but small towns are their own jury, and he became a pariah. He returned to his job as lighthouse keeper, sitting at the edge of Gore Bay, alone with his guilt and melancholy. The weeks stretched to years. A decade after the tragedy, he was seen getting into his boat late in the evening. The next day, the boat was found empty in the bay. Robert's body was discovered floating by the dock. His death was listed as accidental drowning, but the local verdict, the one whispered in the grocery stores and in the harbour, was that he had taken his own life. His son, David Boyter, moved to Little Current, married and had three children. His daughter Violet grew up to marry Morland Ritchie, Harold's brother. David had had both feet amputated, though ironically ran a shoe repair and boot-making business on Water Street.

However fascinated by the salesmen who came through town, Harold's first job wasn't in retail. Despite his exam-stealing antics in his final year (or perhaps because of them), he worked as a school teacher in neighbouring Bidwell, about twenty kilometres away. It was a one-room schoolhouse that included all grades. One of the students was a fifteen-year-old girl named Sarah Jane McArthur, and in the fall of 1900, Harold and Sarah Jane had a relationship. It would have been clandestine, given the times and the circumstances. In late fall, she discovered she was pregnant.

It was one of the most difficult times in Harold's life. In a small town, at the turn of the twentieth century, a sixteen-year-old schoolgirl impregnated by her teacher was even more scandalous than it would be now. While it wasn't illegal (the age of consent was fourteen at that time), it would have been viewed as unethical and, on an island dotted with churches, sinful for both parties. The McArthur and Ritchie families had a shared stake in keeping it a secret, not an easy thing in a small town (population 728 at the time). One of the standard solutions when a man had "gotten a girl in trouble" was for her to leave the island and live with a relative until she could give birth and give the child up for adoption. But that didn't happen in this case. Sarah Jane stayed home and gave birth on the island.

For Harold, it meant the end of his teaching career. The year 1901 wasn't a good one for him. He had the weight of Sarah's situation on his mind and then, on February 28, *The Expositor* reported, "All will regret to hear that Mrs. W.D. Ritchie met with a painful accident from a fall on the sidewalk this week. We understand she is unable to put any weight on her foot as a result." Harold's father, meanwhile, had issues in the lumber world. In April, *The Expositor* reported that "Mr. W.D. Ritchie was over to Square Bay this week scaling some 50,000 logs over which there is a dispute."

CARLOAD RITCHIE

Other members of the Ritchie family fared better. Harold's sister, Mary Lavinia, who had recently married Ruthven Hay, got a cheerful mention in the paper that spring: "Mr. and Mrs. Ruthven Hay entertained a number of the young folk at their residence Sunday evening." And regardless of the family troubles, advertisements for Ritchie's Store continued to run most weeks: "We carry the choicest stock of Groceries, Confectionary, Fresh Bread . . . our prices are the lowest." In the Local & Personal section, the Ritchies ran notices reading "send in your orders for your fine cakes," and "we pay cash to farmers for produce." Harold, meanwhile, lived in torment.

Sarah Jane gave birth on June 20, 1901. The birth record identifies the child only as "Boy Ritchie," a reference to the child's gender rather than a given name. It isn't known what became of the boy. He would have been adopted, but it isn't clear by whom. Sarah Jane had older sisters who were certainly a possibility for adoption, but there is no Boy Ritchie in the genealogical records of any of their families. Neither set of grandparents took the boy in. Nor was there an orphanage on the island.

Harold left the island that year. Sarah Jane went on to marry a man named George Chatwell in December 1905, in nearby Manitowaning. There is no news in *The Expositor* about the wedding, perhaps because Sarah Jane was five-months pregnant at the time. While she was settling into her newlywed life, Harold returned to Little Current for Christmas. On December 21, *The*

Expositor reported that "Harold Ritchie arrived home Saturday and will spend his Christmas vacation here."

Another family member, Harold's brother-in-law Ruthven, became a greater presence in his life around this time. Ruthven operated the town's jail, and he had his hands full the week of Harold's visit with a man who had been arrested for drunkenness and charged with "smashing up the jail" (he was fined by a magistrate). The jail, with a twelve-foot fence around it, sat in Ruthven and Lavinia's backyard on Campbell Street. The Little Current jail was usually occupied. In the course of a year, Ruthven counted forty-eight inmates (forty-three for drunkenness, three for theft, one for beating his wife, and one for breaking out of jail). Lavinia cooked meals for the prisoners.

Ruthven also had a job with B.H. Turner, one of Ritchie's main competitors in the grocery business. Turner owned the island's phone system, and part of Ruthven's job was to walk the wires when there were problems with the telephone cables. He could sometimes hear music coming from the wires. He was a musical man, playing cello in a dance band, and he was the choir leader in the church. Lavinia was the organist (much later, Harold would donate an organ to the church).

William Ritchie had built a hall at the back of his store to host events, and on December 28 a Christmas entertainment was held there, featuring a cantata titled "Santa Claus' Dream." Harold, Lavinia, Ruthven, and the family all attended.

CARLOAD RITCHIE

A week later, Harold's departure was duly recorded in the paper: "Harold Ritchie, who has been spending his Christmas vacation at home, left yesterday for Toronto to resume his duties travelling."

In fact, after the scandal of Sarah Jane's first pregnancy, Harold had moved to Toronto with the intention of improving his education. "I decided to go further with my studies and possibly take up civil engineering, more from the standpoint of learning organization," he told a reporter for the *Toronto Telegram* in a rare interview (the rarity perhaps explained by the scandal hidden in his past). For an ambitious young man of twenty, having spent almost the whole of his life on the island, Toronto must have offered more excitement and opportunity, not to mention the chance of a fresh start. But instead of going to university, Harold got a job as a commissioned salesman. He told the *Telegram*:

> I had an idea of doing business on commission. There was always the possibility that this might not work out, and while I was young, an engineering education could be easily acquired, and might someday be something to fall back on. But I met an old friend, Mr. Wingrove, the owner of the Capstan Manufacturing Company, a man who manufactured baking powder, mince-meat, ground spice, and several lines. He had just lost his northern salesman, so he hired me for a small salary and started me north.

On Harold's first sales trip through northern Ontario, he picked up surprisingly large orders, far more than his predecessor had managed. "I gained the name 'Carload Ritchie' through picking up some rather large orders on my first trip, and while there were some old-time travellers who thought I was a young salesman telling a lot of funny stories and even went so far as to offer to bet with me, I was able to produce the carload orders and the name 'Carload Ritchie' has stuck to me all my life."

With his new income, Harold opened a bank account in Toronto. "My first bank account was started by force," he said. "I went to the Market branch, Canadian Bank of Commerce, with a cheque for $728. I mentioned to the teller that I was going to the races. Mr. T. A. Chisholm, the manager, overheard this. He called me into his office, started to give me advice, and, like a fresh young lad, I resented it, but he stood his ground. He gave me $28 and a bank book for $700, and said, 'Come in to see me Monday.'"

Harold lost his $28 at the races and lost his expense money as well. He went in to see T. A. Chisholm on Monday and continued to bank at the Commerce throughout his life. They remained close friends.

Earning a modest salary, Harold quickly realized that he was worth more than he was being paid. He asked Wingrove for a raise. Wingrove went to see Chisholm at the Bank of Commerce, who advised him to pay Harold more or risk losing him. Wingrove replied, "The young fellow will be too fresh if I pay him what he is worth." As a result, Harold left Capstan Manufacturing and decided to sell independently and solely on commission. It was potentially much more lucrative, but it was also riskier. He was giving up his safety net. "It took a lot of deciding," Harold said, "but I finally did it. I left the Capstan people and started out on my own, taking lines to sell on commission. It was not so easy at first. But more lines meant more commissions, and most important, a reduction in costs."

He was right in theory, but the reality on the ground was a challenge. "The early days were very hard sledding," Harold said, "and on my first trip in western Canada, on my way home from the coast, it took me three weeks to travel from Medicine Hat to Toronto and I did it on $67. One of the misfortunes of the early days was that I represented a large Toronto house and I sold a great deal of merchandise for them on that trip, expecting to come home and find a handsome cheque waiting for me. I got less than 10 percent of what I had earned. The market in England had gone up and they shipped their goods to England and forgot about the young lad who had spent his time and money to sell their goods and introduce them where they had never had any business before."

The prairies that Ritchie travelled across had only recently been filled, many of them immigrants lured by the promise of free land. When Clifford Sifton became the minister of the interior under Liberal Prime Minister Wilfrid Laurier, his main goal had been to populate the west. He was successful: between 1896 and 1914, the population of the prairies went from 300,000 to 1.5 million. The promise of free land (160 acres) wasn't the only enticement. Sifton launched publicity campaigns in foreign papers extolling the charms of the west, using the loose promises of modern advertising. Winters were "bracing" and "invigorating." The climate was "the healthiest in the world." "The frontier of Manitoba is about the same latitude as Paris." While the very southern part of Manitoba (the border with Minnesota) is, in fact, at the same latitude as Paris, no one would confuse the Parisienne winter with Winnipeg's. A narrative was created in ads and pamphlets, painting a picture of another, better life. "The future citizen of the North-West of Canada will have Norse, Celtic, and Saxon blood in his veins. His countenance in the *pure, dry* electric air, will be fresh as the morning. His muscles will be iron, his nerves steel. Vigor will characterize his every action."

Ritchie would later employ some of the same tactics in his own business enterprises. He embodied the vigorous boosterism rampant on the prairies. Those who came west around the turn of the twentieth century were quick to declare that their town, city, territory, was the best of any around. In Winnipeg, the youngest city in the country in 1911 (only 1.5 percent of its citizens were over sixty-five), boosterism was particularly rampant. Saskatoon grandly declared itself "the fastest growing city in the world," "the Largest City in the World for its Age," and "the greatest example of town and city planning in the world's history." Medicine Hat was "the Minneapolis of Canada." Rudyard Kipling, who visited Medicine Hat, went further, calling it the "New Ninevah" with "all hell for a basement." Selkirk, Lethbridge, and Strathcona all announced that they were vital hubs. Cities denigrated other cities in order to attract immigrants: "Girls cannot live morally in Calgary," declared the Regina *Leader Post*.

Travelling through the prairies selling his wares, Ritchie was perfectly attuned to the zeitgeist. He was a booster both of Toronto and Canada. He had an infectious energy that boosters everywhere would recognize. He sold more than his competitors, but he was hounded by bad luck. "Another of the firms for whom I started out in the commission business failed when I was halfway west. I have never forgotten, when hiring salesmen, some of the hardships of a salesman, and it was possibly a good lesson, and has helped me a great deal."

Harold realized he had to get on with larger, more stable firms. "At that time, I represented some small houses, but gradually acquired larger houses. At that time the Imperial Extract Company gave a great help by allowing me to be their sales agent for many years." The Imperial Extract Company sold Shirriff Marmalade among other products, and was known across the country, but Harold was able to expand their Canadian business.

His early observation about representing more than one line became one of the founding principles of his sales empire. But

Western Canada had limitations as a sales territory. Despite the boom in immigration, the population was still quite small, and it was spread over millions of square miles. It was difficult and expensive to get around. He was as successful as he could be in that territory, and it wasn't enough. He realized he'd have to go farther afield if he wanted to expand his business. He either needed more territory or more lines to sell.

In 1905, at the age of twenty-four, Harold went to London, England, and met with the firm of Samuel Hanson and Son, at the time the largest wholesale grocer in the world. It was an audacious act for a young man. Transatlantic travel was both slow and expensive, and it was an investment in time and money that had little real chance of success. But he wanted to represent Samuel Hanson in Canada, and he convinced them that he knew the Canadian market better than anyone else. "Mr. Tanner, the managing director, later said, through the nerve or what might be called in this country, ego, which I displayed, he gave me his line, and the firm of Samuel Hanson and Son helped to put me on my feet. I sold hundreds of carloads of green coffee, rice, tea, Malaga grapes, Spanish onions, pearl barley, split peas and general lines." These lines quickly made up the backbone of Harold's business.

In 1906, he returned to England. After his initial success with Samuel Hanson, Ritchie hoped to represent the J.C. Eno company, which was also based in England. Their signature product was Eno's Fruit Salts, an antacid that alleviated indigestion (although it made other claims, as well). He tried to see the owner about representing him in Canada and couldn't get a meeting. He returned a year later and called three times. The firm finally relented and Harold got a meeting with a manager who told him they weren't interested in selling their product in Canada on commission. At the time, Eno was a huge company, recognized in a dozen countries. The manager would be looking at a short young man who had no real sales network, talking about how he would increase Eno's business in a country that had less than a quarter of Britain's population, spread over an area almost eighty times the size of England. It was hard to see the upside.

"I finally made a proposition that I would double their business in Canada or no pay," Harold said. "They took me up. I not only doubled it but gave them four times the business the first year." Eno assumed he had saturated the market, and sales would be poor the following year. But Harold doubled the business again in his next campaign and was given a handsome bonus. He returned to London again in the fall of 1907, looking for more English lines.

Harold's success as a salesman was now cemented. He was finally ready to get married and settle down. In 1908, he married Alice Alberta Brydon, although he never settled down.

CHAPTER TWO

Alice Alberta

ALICE ALBERTA BRYDON, known as Berta throughout her life, had also lived in Little Current. The path taken by the Brydon family was similar to that of the Ritchies: Scottish roots and the hope of greater opportunity in the New World. Berta's father, Archibald Brydon, was born at Aberlosk, in Dumfriesshire, Scotland, and came to Canada at the age of four. His father, David Bryden, had been a small-hold tenant in Dumfriesshire, working land that belonged to the Duke of Buccleugh. David left Scotland in 1847 because the lease on the farm expired. To the north, the Highland Clearances had already resulted in the removal of most tenant farmers, and small tenant farmers everywhere in Scotland were being taken over by larger farms. The future was bleak. At the same time, immigration was a risk, especially since David's wife, Janet Glendenning Brydon, was pregnant, and they already had four children under the age of seven. When they arrived in Upper Canada, the Brydons stayed with Janet's brother Sandy, who was living in Scarborough, at the time a distance from the town of York, later Toronto. York was still three years away from incorporating as a township, and is described by historian Michael Kluckner as "a parochial and fastidious place, inbred and gossip-prone, with a ruling clique whose fingers were in every pie from government through mercantilism."

The Brydons finally settled in Waterloo County, in the town of Galt, which was then "for all practical purposes a Scottish town." David wrote to his brother, "Go into Galt and you cannot fail to see some old acquaintances [from Scotland] and get a hearty welcome." David continued the farming he had done in Scotland.

In 1869, his son Archibald, a carpenter, moved to Berlin, Ontario (now Kitchener—the name changed during the First World War due to anti-German sentiment). The following year he was in Hespeler (adjacent to Galt; both towns are now part of the city of Cambridge). By 1881, he was in Muskoka, and had gone from carpenter to sawmill owner. Berta was born in 1882, in Gravenhurst (Norman Bethune would be born in that same town eight years later). In 1885, the Anton Mill, which was north of Barrie, was torn down and moved to Little Current. Archibald became the foreman of what was now called the Red Mill, the very mill that Harold's father had first worked at when he arrived on Manitoulin. They would certainly have known one another. Archibald built a house for his family in 1886. Eventually, there were five children: Edith, Walter, Alice, Alberta, Margaret, and Mabel.

Harold's family had been linked to tragedy on Manitoulin, and the Brydons had some bad luck of their own. In 1886, when Berta's brother Walter was thirteen-years-old, he went hunting with an older neighbour, Bryan MacKie, who owned a hotel in Little Current, as well as a saloon on the waterfront and a tugboat. The two were in a duck blind when they heard birds flying overhead. They rushed to take their positions and Walter's gun went off. His bird shot hit Bryan, who collapsed and lay wounded in the bush. Walter likely went to get help, but Bryan died several days later of his wounds. The death certificate said he died of blood poisoning, the result of the lead bird shot.

Eight years later, the twenty-one-year-old Walter married Bryan's daughter Jane. They had a son, but the marriage didn't last. It couldn't have been a happy union as Walter, at its end, declared he would go as far away as possible. He moved to British Columbia. In the 1901 census, Jane describes herself as a widow, although Walter was still alive. They were finally divorced in 1924, and Walter remarried that year. Berta stayed in touch with Walter and visited him on the coast. Harold would sometimes accompany her, checking in with his west coast sales team. There are photographs of Harold sitting in a car in front of a massive redwood tree in what may be Vancouver's Stanley Park.

CARLOAD RITCHIE

In the 1890s, the US imposed tariffs on Canadian lumber, something that would become a recurring theme over the next 130 years. As a result, the Red Mill had little business. By 1901, the year Harold left town, the Brydon family had returned to Hespeler. Berta trained to be a schoolteacher, one of the few professions available to women at the time. She distinguished herself quickly, and in 1902, at the age of twenty, she was one of forty Canadian teachers selected to go to South Africa to teach English to Boer women and children in British concentration camps.

The Boer War had begun as a lesson in British imperial might, and ended as a grim and bloody mess. It began in October 1899, and was fought between the British and two Boer states: the South African Republic, and the Orange Free State. It was viewed by many, both within and outside of Britain, as simply a war of imperialism. The British thought it would be a short, decisive battle, "over by Christmas." Instead, it was an ugly, protracted guerilla war that claimed the lives of 22,000 British soldiers, with more of them dying of disease than in battle.

To combat the guerilla tactics of the Boers, the British initiated a scorched earth policy, burning farms, killing livestock, and putting the civilian population, most of them women and children, in badly run concentration camps. By the war's end, more than 28,000 Boer civilians had died in the camps, mostly of famine or disease, 22,000 of them children. As well, 15,000

Africans died in the camps. John McCrae, the Canadian who went on to write the poem, "In Flanders Fields," during the First World War, was part of the Boer War effort. He had been eager to go, seduced by Rudyard Kipling's romantic notion of war and empire, but he grew disillusioned after he arrived. "For absolute neglect and rotten administration, it is a model," he wrote of the debacle. "I am ashamed of some members of my profession. . . . The soldier's game is not what it's cracked up to be." British victory came with international censure. When news of the disastrous camps got back to London, many Brits were appalled. While some still viewed victory as a glorious success, others saw it as a stain on the empire.

Whichever view was taken, it left a bitter colony in its wake. Alfred Milner, the British High Commissioner for Southern Africa, was charged with the task of managing the territory. He embarked on a plan of reconstruction that lasted from 1902 to 1910. At the heart of the plan was the development of the massive gold deposits and the exclusion of the Black majority from political power. Milner also wanted a country politically dominated by English-speaking whites, but he was unable to attract British immigrants. His back-up plan was to teach the Afrikaner population to speak English, to make the Boers "British in one generation."

To this end, 300 women teachers from Canada, Britain, Australia, and New Zealand were recruited to teach English to the women and children still held in British concentration camps. More than 500 Canadian women applied and only forty were chosen, among them Berta Brydon. They chose the best and brightest, women who "fit the ideal of Canadian and Imperial womanhood" (Roman Catholics were excluded). They signed a contract for a year and were paid 100 pounds sterling.

Berta sailed from Halifax aboard the *Corinthian* on April 12, 1902, and docked in England. Before setting out for South Africa, she and the other teachers spent ten days in London. They visited the colonial office and had tea with the British aristocracy, including Earl Grey, the governor general. They sat through speeches about the importance of their work and the glory of the empire. Berta attended a session of the House of Commons and was surprised to see the honourable members visibly bored, their feet up on desks, reading newspapers or openly talking with one another, while a speaker droned on about a ways-and-means bill. It looked like a room filled with badly behaved schoolchildren, not the fount of parliamentary democracy. The volunteer teachers toured the city, took in the famous sights, and bought the school supplies they would need before sailing for the Cape.

They arrived in Africa and took the train from Cape Town to the camps. The war had officially ended on May 31, only two days before they arrived, and the signs of battle were everywhere. From the train, the women saw barbed wire, blockhouses with sandbags around them, and large cemeteries filled with uniform white crosses. In places there were scattered graves and bones bleaching in the sun, empty tins, dead cattle. A column of ragged soldiers straggled past. The dust settled like snow.

The teachers were scattered around the country. There is a photograph of Berta standing in front of the Modderfontein School, a handsome brick building. Modderfontein was a small mining town near the Mud River (Modderfontein translates as "Muddy Fountain"). Her future husband had only left teaching the year before, after two years at the one-room schoolhouse in Bidwell. Berta stayed in South Africa for two years.

It isn't clear if the 300 women who came to teach were exposed to the worst of the camps, which were scenes of squalor, misery, and death. The camps were dusty, hot, and lacked the most basic amenities. Typhoid, malaria, and pneumonia were rampant. It was a dangerous place to be, and the sheer inhumanity would be a shock to someone coming from placid Ontario.

The photographs from South Africa show a more genteel existence. Berta is seen with a friend, wearing a sunbonnet and a long dress, holding a tennis racquet. The first school she taught at looks like it could be in any small town in Ontario.

There was a teachers' convention in Johannesburg, where all the commonwealth teachers convened. A city of about 60,000 then, the streets of Johannesburg were covered in red dust. The women visited Pretoria, toured a gold mine, and attended a garden party hosted by Lord Milner. King Edward's coronation happened while they were there, and they took part in the celebrations, which were boycotted by the Boers.

In the end, Milner's reconstruction plans failed. Instead of making the Boers British through compulsory anglicization, he fuelled Afrikaner nationalism. "Milnerism," as it was called in South Africa, was a dirty word. If Milner's social ambitions failed, he was successful in raising profits from the gold mines, albeit at the expense of Black labour. His policies set the stage for future conflicts that played out over the next century.

* * *

The South African camps made a profound impression on Berta. Disease was rampant there and in the military hospitals, and she was appalled at the death toll. When she returned to Canada, she started training as a nurse at Toronto General Hospital. She was a tall, elegant woman who now carried the confidence of someone who had gone abroad, and who had succeeded at a difficult task at a young age—someone who was ready to do good in the world.

In July 1903, while Berta was in South Africa, Harold was aboard a steamship, the *Emma*, at Rose Point on Parry Island in Georgian Bay. He was still a salesman for the Capstan Manufacturing Company at the time, making his rounds of northern Ontario. As the steamer pulled away, a twelve-year-old girl named Lena Shepherd fell off the wharf, into the water.

Her father, the stationmaster, instinctively jumped in to save her. Shepherd couldn't swim, however, and went down before resurfacing and going down again. Harold, who had grown up on the water and was a capable swimmer, took off his boots and jacket and dove in. He was able to bring Shepherd back to the surface. The man was unconscious, but Harold kept his head above water and got him to shore. Lena made it to shore, as well, with the help of others. A doctor on a camping trip happened to be at the scene and was able to resuscitate Shepherd. Harold was given a Royal Humane Society medal, his bravery written up glowingly in the newspapers.

Harold would have known Berta from Manitoulin. It was a small town, and their fathers certainly would have known one another from the mill. Harold and Berta reunited in Toronto, either in 1904 or 1905, when Berta was training as a nurse at Toronto General. She graduated in 1906 and worked as superintendent of nurses at Kenora and at the Royal Victoria Hospital in Barrie. On November 10, 1908, she and Harold were married by the Reverend George Wesley Robinson, who they knew from Manitoulin, at the Davisville Methodist Church on Yonge Street.

As a bachelor, Harold had lived for a time in an apartment at 50 Jarvis Street. In 1905, he was staying at the Grand Central Hotel on Simcoe Street. Because he travelled so much, it may have made sense simply to stay in a hotel when in Toronto, rather than pay for an apartment that would sit empty most of the time.

CARLOAD RITCHIE

Now wed, he and Berta needed a permanent address. They moved into the Queen's Court apartments at 579 Jarvis Street, near Bloor. It had been built that year and contained thirteen apartments. It was a graceful building, and the location was enviable, among the grand homes of Jarvis. A canopy of old-growth trees covered the street. Allan Gardens was nearby, one of the city's most graceful parks. Their daughter Dorothy was born at Queen's Court in 1909. Two years later, the family moved into a house on Deer Park Crescent, north of St. Clair Avenue, west of Yonge Street, where their daughters Kathleen and Pauline were both born.

Berta quit nursing to raise the children, but soon became active both as a volunteer and, later, a financial supporter of the Children's Aid Society and St. John Ambulance. She was one of the founders of the social service department at Toronto General Hospital, and involved in the establishment of the St. John Convalescent Hospital in Willowdale. As Harold's fortunes increased, so did Berta's philanthropy. She had done the two professional jobs available to women at the time—teaching and nursing—and had distinguished herself at both. She would go on to take a job that very few women had.

CHAPTER THREE

The Travelling Salesman

THE TURN OF THE CENTURY was a good time to be a salesman. Both Canada and the city of Toronto were undergoing a boom that lasted from 1896 to 1913. Part of the expansion was due to the settlement of the west and a growing market in agricultural products. Toronto had become a manufacturing base, employing more than 50,000 people, and immigrants continued to flock to Canada from abroad. The country was rapidly urbanizing (in 1901, 35 percent of the population lived in an urban area; by 1911, it was 42 percent). Toronto was dotted with fine churches, and its dominant forces, religion and capitalism, were sometimes difficult to tell apart. The ruling Methodists had business and political ties, a network of intermarriage and interfaith commerce that ran through the city. Harold was a Presbyterian but rarely attended services (he would have been surprised to learn that one of his granddaughters, Victoria Matthews, would become Canada's first female Anglican bishop). The Methodists believed sinners could achieve perfection through repentance. The Presbyterians believed that being Presbyterian wouldn't stop you from sinning, but it would stop you from enjoying it.

Harold took advantage of the boom. His connections in London with Samuel Hanson and Eno led to selling other English lines. England had a vigorous export business, and English goods were coveted in Canada. "I gradually acquired other English lines of merchandise," Harold said. "Then I was told I could work in the United States for some of these lines." By 1910, he had significantly expanded both the lines he represented and the territories he covered.

Exceptionally successful as a salesman, Harold made a good income. When he returned to Little Current in 1910, he brought his new touring car, described in *The Expositor* as "of magnificent proportions." There is a photograph in the paper of Harold and his mother sitting in the car, which would have been a novelty in Little Current then.

Still working out of a small office in the Queen City Chambers on Church Street, Harold realized he would need to expand. In 1911, he decided to build an office rather than rent more space in an established building. He bought land on McCaul Street,

THE TRAVELLING SALESMAN

just above Queen Street, outside the traditional downtown area where most offices were, and therefore less expensive. It wasn't the last time that Harold would choose to locate outside the mainstream. "I had bought the land at a very reasonable price," he said, "but it was a considerable struggle. I didn't have any backing and had to make money and pay as I went. I travelled and earned money and paid for the building under construction out of my earnings." It was a graceful building designed by Charles MacKay Willmot, with help from Harold. On the second floor, he had a small mahogany-panelled office with a large mahogany desk and opulent carpets. He was rarely in the office, however. He preferred to be out on the floor, selling.

That year, he formed an Ontario chartered company with William Millsap, S. G. Amaden, and L.W. McWaters called International Proprietaries Ltd. The new company had some growing pains. "I did not make as much money for some time after I formed my business into a company as I had made previously," he said, "because we had extra expenses and the men with me were not accustomed to selling several lines and it took some time for them to start to earn money. However, our business steadily grew."

As business expanded, Harold travelled more frequently. In the fall of 1911, he went to England aboard the *Megantic*, returning in early December. The following year, he returned to England in April, this time in the company of Berta. It took more

CARLOAD RITCHIE

than a week just to cross the Atlantic then, and his overseas trips always lasted a month or more. Harold began taking his family with him whenever possible. On November 20, 1913, he, Berta, and their daughter Dorothy, who was four at the time, sailed from Quebec to Liverpool aboard the *Empress of Ireland*. First class accommodation was on the upper deck, which had its own private promenade. There was also a music room with a grand piano, something Harold may have taken advantage of. There was a separate dining room for children. For those who could afford it, travel was a grand affair. Steamer trunks were huge and beautifully crafted, lined with silk, brass and mahogany (vintage Louis Vuitton steamer trunks from the 1920s sell for more than $50,000 now). Some of them could be stood up vertically and opened to reveal five drawers on one side and a rack to hang clothes on the other.

From Liverpool, the family went to London, where Harold had meetings with Eno and with Samuel Hanson and others. There isn't a record of where they stayed, but in later years Harold always stayed at the Ritz Hotel on Piccadilly. On December 18, the family sailed from Liverpool to New York on board the *SS Cedric*, then took the train back to Toronto.

Four months after they had been on the *Empress of Ireland*, it was involved in the largest peacetime disaster in Canadian history. Sailing from North America to Europe, the ship's upper decks usually were filled with prosperous travelers who wanted to tour the continent. On return voyages, its upper deck was rarely full while steerage was overcrowded with immigrants looking for a better life in the new world. On March 29, 1914, the *Empress of Ireland* collided with a Norwegian coal ship in the mouth of the St. Lawrence River. It was night and there was a thick fog. The *Empress of Ireland* sank quickly. Of the 1,477 people on board, 1,012 died, many of them children.

Harold's company had a few very good years before the disruption of the First World War. "When war broke out, we got a terrible jolt," Harold said. "Our English lines were cut off. Everything was topsy-turvy. The exchange was shot to pieces and one of our great pieces of earning power was gone. In fact, we never regained the business we had with Samuel Hanson and Son."

Instead, Harold looked south. He got more American agencies, expanding both the lines he represented and his sales network. As he expanded, however, the world began to contract. The year before the war began, Canada was hit by a recession shared by most of the developed world. The boom that had lasted seventeen years was over. Factories were closing, there were fewer jobs, fewer consumers, and markets were depressed. There was drought on the prairies.

Also, the world was rapidly changing. It was the age of the automobile, the age of flight. Telephones and electricity were spreading. The first radio transmission had been sent across the Atlantic Ocean. These weren't the only innovations. The weapons of war had also advanced, and their destructive power would soon take the world by surprise.

When Britain declared war on Germany on August 4, 1914, Canada, as a colony, was automatically entered in the conflict along with the rest of the empire. In the Battle of Ypres, Canadian soldiers were the first to experience the horrors of modern warfare when a heavy green-yellow cloud of gas descended on them, the birth of chemical warfare. The chlorine gas caused hideous injuries and was impossible to defend against.

The war did not stop Harold from continuing to sail to London. His first trip had him arriving in Liverpool on November 17, 1914, and staying in London until mid-December. Three months later, Germany announced that they considered the seas around the British Isles to be a war zone; after February 18, 1915, they would sink any Allied ship in the area, whether military or civilian. In May, a German U-boat hit the *Lusitania* with a torpedo. It was making passage to Liverpool. The ship went down quickly and 1,198 lives were lost. Despite the threats to merchant ships, Harold sailed from New York to Liverpool on the *Baltic*, in December 1915. He stayed in London until December 29, then returned to New York.

London was a dangerous place to be. In May 1915, Germany launched the first of its aerial attacks on the city. An ominous, 650-foot-long Zeppelin drifted over London, opened a trapdoor, and dropped ninety incendiary bombs and thirty grenades on sleeping Londoners. It marked a turning point in the war, one where civilians were legitimate targets. "Modern warfare is total warfare," warned the German zeppelin commander, Peter Strasser. On September 8, 1915, a zeppelin dropped a three-ton bomb on London, the largest yet. Dubbed "baby-killers" by the British, the zeppelins terrorized London for almost two years.

Harold returned to London in July 1916, staying at the Berkeley Hotel for two weeks before returning to New York. He was still living at Deer Park Crescent at that point, and on the ship's manifest, he is listed as a "broker" with an identification mark: "sore on right ankle." On a later voyage, it's listed as a "scar on the right ankle." This may have been the result of a dog bite. Harold had a Jack Russell terrier named Beni (named for Beniamino Gigli, the Italian opera singer). Harold loved the dog, although he was alone in this, and his love was unrequited. The dog bit everyone, including Harold. It finally ran away, its absence mourned only by Harold.

Little more than a month after Harold left London, the zeppelin threat abated somewhat. On October 1, 1916, Germany's most successful airship commander, Heinrich Mathy, had flown over London. A Saskatchewan farmer with the enviable fighter-pilot name of Wulstan Tempest went up in an experimental aircraft and attacked it with newly developed incendiary bullets. The zeppelin, filled with highly flammable hydrogen, exploded.

The remains landed in the field of another farmer, north of London. He charged people one shilling to come to his property to view the wreckage.

In 1917, Harold once more went to London for three weeks, this time in the summer. Before he arrived the Germans bombed London with fixed-wing aircraft. The advent of incendiary bullets had cost Germany more than half its fleet of zeppelins, necessitating the deployment of biplanes. They roared over the London skies, dropping bombs. While lacking the ominous, futuristic menace of the zeppelins, they were ultimately more destructive. In June, a daylight raid resulted in 162 deaths.

The chances of being caught in a bombing raid were statistically quite low, but crossing the Atlantic was a gamble every time. German U-boats patrolled the shipping lanes and were deadly and hard to defend against. By the end of the war, they had sunk almost 5,000 ships. Harold's family didn't accompany him on any of his wartime visits, but he continued to take his chances. He believed in the power of personal contact; it was the bedrock of his sales empire and the war wasn't going to stop that.

At home, the war economy lifted the country out of the economic depression. And with so many men away fighting, Canadian women took the opportunity to make a case against the evils of alcohol. As a result, prohibition hit the country, starting with Saskatchewan in 1915. All other provinces jumped on the bandwagon the following year, with the lone exception, unsurprisingly, of Quebec. In 1917, Canadians distinguished themselves at Vimy, driving the Germans back from the ridge, something the British and French armies had been unable to do. The cost was steep: 3,598 Canadians dead and 7,004 wounded in four days of bitter fighting. But Vimy was a watershed that not only helped unite a country still divided over the war, but also helped define it.

In 1916, Prime Minister Robert Borden named Toronto businessman Joseph Flavelle, head of the Imperial Munitions Board and he quickly made it an efficient enterprise. By 1917, Canada was sending almost a third of the shells used by the allies in Europe. King George V made Flavelle a baronet. But it was at this point that Toronto newspapers revealed that Flavelle, who had made much of his fortune in canned salt pork, had made record profits by selling bacon to the English. *Saturday Night* magazine accused Flavelle of creating an artificial shortage to drive up the price of pork ("the most sordid and despicable trafficking, namely the accumulation of great wealth out of the blood and agony of those who fight in the trenches.") He was asked to resign from the munitions board, but refused. He was exonerated by a royal commission, but not by the public. His food enterprises showed profits of 80 percent, and the play this got in the newspapers was enough to brand him a profiteer in the public imagination.

Harold bought a grand house at 40 Burton Road in Forest Hill Village in 1916. The land occupied the better part of a city block.

It had three storeys, with a garage, servant quarters, and extensive gardens. Eventually, Harold added the gate that had survived the demolition of Benvenuto, the residence of S.H. James, a Toronto real estate developer. James had the intricate wrought-iron gates made in Italy when he and his family were visiting on vacation. His mansion was demolished in 1931, and the gates and Kingston stone piers to which they were attached were moved to Harold's property. In his book *Toronto, No Mean City*, Eric Arthur wrote, "there were are no finer examples of wrought iron in Canada."

The house on Burton Road was filled with people, Harold rarely one of them. He was travelling extensively, across the country, through the US, away for up to nine months of the year. Berta had her two sisters, Margaret and Mabel, living with her. Margaret helped run the household. Mabel was stricken with myasthenia gravis, a disease where there is a breakdown in communication between nerves and muscles, resulting in chronic weakness, difficulty with speech, and trouble swallowing and breathing. It was what killed their mother, and Mabel was largely bedridden—an invalid, in the parlance of the day. Eventually Berta's father, Archibald, would move in with them as well.

It grew into a kind of compound, with Harold's immediate and extended family living nearby. Ruthven Hay and Lavinia lived on Glenayr, a block away. Hal and Dorothy Crang were at 38 Burton Road (later, Berta's sisters, Margaret and Mabel, moved into 38 Burton). Glen Robinson, Berta's nephew, was at

1 Burton Road. Harold's daughter, Kathleen, and her husband, Tom Gilmour, were at 42 Burton Road. It echoed a theme that was part of Harold's life: keeping friends and family near, both at home and in business.

At the time, Forest Hill Village wasn't part of Toronto. The city of Toronto had gone on an annexation spree that started in the 1880s, but Forest Hill Village wasn't part of the plan. Its undulating, complicated topography and sparse population (500 people in 1910) made it an uninviting target. It had Upper Canada College, The Bishop Strachan School, and some grand residences, but it was essentially a country village, and there were still dairy farms in operation. This may have been part of the appeal for both Harold and Berta: echoes of small-town life amid the grand homes. In 1923, it incorporated officially as Forest Hill Village. Among its early bylaws was the stipulation that only residential structures could be built, and these could only be detached or semi-detached homes. No apartments were allowed, the beginnings of its exclusivity.

While some of the city's elite were still living on Jarvis and Sherbourne Streets, others were moving north to Rosedale where there was a ravine to separate them from the soot and bustle of downtown. Some residents went still farther north and west, into what is now Forest Hill. This slow exodus was the beginning of the decline of Jarvis and Sherbourne streets, its Second Empire mansions eventually devolving into rooming houses.

CARLOAD RITCHIE

To the south of the Ritchie home, E. J. Lennox, the architect who designed the old City Hall, designed a home for financier Henry Pellatt. His massive folly, Casa Loma, took three years to build, starting in 1911, and was finished in time for the war. It had ninety-eight rooms and was almost 65,000 square feet. By 1923, Pellatt was essentially broke and his castle was seized by the city for unpaid taxes.

The other grand home in the area was Sir John Craig Eaton's mansion on Davenport Road, just east of Casa Loma. Eaton, heir to the Timothy's department store empire, met his wife, Flora McCrea, in Rotherham House, a private hospital on Sherbourne Street, where she was a nurse and he was trying not to drink. Eaton died in 1922 at the age of forty-six, and Lady Eaton (her husband had been knighted in 1915) became the director of the corporation. She scheduled board meetings for Tuesdays because she liked to stay in bed on Mondays. Their fifty-room mansion, Ardworld, which included a private hospital, didn't have a long life span. It was torn down in 1936. Lady Eaton was allegedly the first woman in Canada to drive a car, and the first to have an accident.

Despite the fact that he was rarely home, Harold took an active interest in the politics of Forest Hill Village. In 1925, he invited fifty councillors and residents to a banquet in the Yellow Room at the King Edward Hotel, his preferred venue for any event when he was in town. The village had an operating surplus, enough to add four rooms to the school and pay all the teachers. At the meeting, they decided a volunteer fire department would be a good idea.

They had only one policeman, a man named Gordon Fraser, who had been rejected by the Toronto police force for being too short. His house on Coulson Avenue also served as the police station. There wasn't much use for it, however, as crime was minor and infrequent. The village nevertheless claimed a connection to one of the biggest crimes of the decade. In 1934, John Labatt, heir to the beer fortune, was kidnapped on the road between Sarnia and London. The nabbing created such a press furore that the kidnappers panicked and, without waiting for a payoff, dumped Labatt, blindfolded, in Forest Hill Village, where he was discovered by baffled passersby.

Near the end of the war, Harold cemented his expansion into the US. He could see that the world order was shifting. America would soon replace Britain as Canada's largest trading partner. "In 1918, we opened our United States office in New York," Harold said. The success of the New York office led to offices in Chicago, Philadelphia, and San Francisco.

In Canada, he opened offices in Montreal, Winnipeg, and Vancouver. There were other Canadian companies with offices across the country, and some even had offices in the US. But Harold was looking around the globe. He expanded to Sydney, Australia; Wellington, New Zealand; Shanghai, Hong Kong, and London, England. He reached into South America, rare at the time, putting offices in Buenos Aires, Rio de Janeiro, Valparaiso, and Lima. He was also in most of Central America and much of the West Indies. "Our company has grown from an Ontario chartered company," Harold said, "to a dominion company in Canada, an incorporated company in the US, and a British company which operates in Australia, New Zealand, and England."

After the war, Spanish Influenza moved around the globe with frightening speed. Spain was the first to report the virus and was saddled with the name, although it likely originated elsewhere. Within a year, it would kill twenty million people, including 55,000 Canadians, almost as many as died in the war (60,000).

It first arrived in Toronto in the spring of 1918, but the second wave, in October, was much deadlier. Toronto had just under a million people then. Toronto's Medical Officer of Health, Charles Hastings, said, "The epidemic struck Toronto almost like a cyclone, assuming epidemic proportions on or about October 9." On October 19, theatres, moving picture shows, pool halls, and other public gathering places were all closed by an order from the city. The hospitals were full. Toronto and much of the world hunkered down to wait out the plague. Harold, a born optimist, felt it would pass, and in its wake there would be pent-up demand. He was moving around the globe at roughly the same rate as the pandemic. He was right about its short duration. As Hastings said, the flu "continued until November 2, when it subsided as rapidly as it began."

In February 1919, Harold again returned to London, staying until the third week of March. He was briefly at home before going back to London, staying until August. At that point, the third wave of the Spanish Flu was moving through Europe. Once again, it was a dangerous time to be travelling, and people were advised to wear masks and stay home.

The Spanish Flu exacerbated what was already a difficult economy. Canada quickly lapsed into recession after the war. Factories closed and it would be three years before the Twenties roared in Canada the way they were roaring in the US. By 1919, the US had replaced Britain as Canada's largest trading partner, and Harold immediately expanded his operations there.

In 1920, he was in New York and London three times. He was back in London in August 1921, sailing on the *Empress of France*. On the ship's manifest, his languages are listed as English, French, and, oddly, Italian, perhaps the result of listening to his favourite opera singer.

By the early 1920s, sales were becoming a dominant aspect of the US corporate ethos. The size of America's manufacturing industry and the mass production of goods led to a change in how sales were conducted. They could no longer rely on itinerant travelling salesmen. Large companies needed their own sales forces, ones that were organized and professional. Sales began to

CARLOAD RITCHIE

take an outsize role, not just in American business, but American culture, as well.

At this point, Harold still had the most globally comprehensive sales force. His only real competition came from John H. Patterson, president of National Cash Register (NCR). Patterson believed in the "science" of sales. He established a sales training academy, created what is believed to be the first sales manual, analyzed territories, set quotas, and wrote detailed sales scripts that his salesmen had to adhere to. By the 1920s, Patterson had developed a global reach. There were three essential differences between Patterson and Harold. The first was that Patterson only had one product: cash registers. The second was that Harold had actually gone farther afield, to parts of South America that NCR hadn't penetrated. And, lastly, there was the dramatic difference in temperament. Patterson was hugely influential in the world of American sales, but he was a tyrant. "He was not a likeable person," said Walter Friedman, author of *Birth of a Salesman*. "He believed in the need to break men down, treat them cruelly at times, and then rebuild them as good agents or executives for NCR."

Harold believed that sales could shape individuals, but his approach was the opposite of Patterson's. "We are very much interested in the development of young men in our business," he said. He wanted to mold them, to change their lives and make them wealthy. He wasn't looking for "one call men," as he called them, salesman who visited the client once. Persistence was a necessary trait for the job, but the two qualities Harold prized most were reliability and good character. "I don't care how well a man can sell if he doesn't have those qualities," Harold said. He hired Canadians to oversee the foreign offices. His strategy was to put them out in the field for two-year stints, enough time to gain an understanding of a foreign territory. Then they would come back and be posted elsewhere. At a time when Canada remained a largely parochial country, Harold created both an international presence and a worldly sales force, all in his own image.

On February 8, 1921, Harold held a sales convention at Toronto's King Edward Hotel. Seventy of his salesmen from around the world attended (fifty others couldn't make it) and the conference went on for a week. For the first two days of the conference, Harold talked about the principles of salesmanship. In later sessions, Mr. Shirriff of the Imperial Extract Company talked to the assembled men about selling marmalade. Other sessions covered Sunset Soap Dye, Alfred Bird & Sons custard powders, Sozodont, Beachnut, Brown's Bronchial Troche, and Eno's Fruit Salts. On Wednesday, they went to the Eaton's Grill Room for lunch. There was a talk about advertising, and Harold took all seventy men to dinner at the King Edward Hotel. They took in a hockey game, saw the sights of Toronto, and then the whole group travelled to New York for more meetings.

By now, there were decades of experience behind Harold's methods. He had witnessed the travelling salesman firsthand as a boy, and had been one. He changed the world of travelling salesmen, making it more efficient by representing more lines. He then created the sales force of the future: professional, organized, sophisticated, armed with marketing savvy. That force, in turn, helped create the consumer society that was fundamental to the American Dream. While America personified the idea of the salesman, and no country was as affected by sales and marketing as the US, the leading expert and most powerful sales figure was a Canadian from a small town on a remote island.

* * *

In late September 1923, Harold, Berta, and their two older daughters, Dorothy and Kathleen, who were thirteen and twelve, sailed from Quebec to Southampton on the *Empress of Britain*, the sister ship of the sunken *Empress of Ireland*. Both ships had been built in Scotland and were owned by Canadian Pacific Steamship. They stayed at the Ritz Hotel, at the time London's most glamourous. Louis Mountbatten was a regular. Hollywood celebrities Charlie Chaplin and Douglas Fairbanks both stayed there, and Noël Coward frequented the restaurant.

Travelling with Harold and his family was John Ross Orr, a director of HFR Co., who was running the Australian operation at the time. Their British lines had expanded, and Harold spent more than a month in London. During these trips Berta sometimes went on to Paris, a city she was fond of. They all returned to New York on November 19 aboard the *Adriatic*.

The following fall, Harold and Berta returned to London for three weeks, this time on their own, without any children in tow. In 1927, they returned to London with three of their daughters, Dorothy, Kathleen and Pauline, once more staying at the Ritz. Travelling with Harold were two HFR Co. employees, John Spence, his secretary, and Noel Marshall. While Harold was away from home for nine months of the year, he was never away from his family for long. Throughout his career, Berta and one or more daughters would be in London, New York, or Vancouver with him.

At home, Toronto was starting to take shape, and to see itself on a grander scale. The Royal Ontario Museum was built in 1914. Union Station and the Royal York Hotel opened their doors in 1927. Eaton's opened its Art Deco department store at College and Yonge streets in 1928. Maple Leaf Gardens followed in 1931 (constructed in under six months, less time than most kitchen renovations). But Toronto's business elite were largely Methodist and their staid stamp was on the city. English writer Wyndham Lewis, who lived in Toronto for several years, described it as "a sanctimonious ice box . . . this bush metropolis of the Orange Lodges." Even Toronto's establishment weren't always fans. Poet Anne Wilkinson, who grew up as part of the Anglican Osler clan in Rosedale, described it as "the home of righteous mediocrity."

But Harold loved the city. "Toronto is a great city," he said.

"There is no place in the world just like it." He saw its potential, envisioning the city as a global hub, the centre of manufacturing, as well as his vast sales empire.

He was largely alone in this vision. Toronto's business class at the time was an insular group. But Harold intended to make Canada a global corporate player. "We believe that Canadians can just as well represent large sums of capital invested in legitimate merchandising as any other people in the world," he said, "and we believe that Canadians can be just as enterprising. We will not go into anything that we do not control, and it is our belief that we can continue to successfully conduct this business and new businesses which may be acquired, and bring to Canada the headquarters of many world-wide institutions."

When challenged on the ability of Canada's banks to back enterprising men, Harold responded, "Any man who will go straight can get all the backing he needs in the Dominion of Canada. Once in a while you hear people say our banks are not enterprising. This is entirely wrong. There is not a crowd of bankers who will back legitimate undertakings and sane business development more quickly than a Canadian bank." Harold had a good relationship with the banks, and his balanced portfolio of assets withstood the early ravages of the depression, unlike many of his peers. There was a growing nationalism after the First World War, a sense of confidence and accomplishment, and Harold personified this moment. But he had even bigger dreams.

Harold Ritchie in 1910, age twenty-nine.

Harold, his family, and friends in 1930 before they sailed on the steamer "Empress of Australia" from New York to London, England.

The Ritchie Store on Manitoulin Island.

Matilda Johnston, wife of William David Ritchie and mother of Lavinia, Harold F., and Morland Ritchie.

Young Berta.

Berta in her wedding dress.

From left to right: Antoinette Ritchie, Pauline Ritchie, Kathleen Ritchie, and Dorothy Ritchie (centre) the bride, at Dorothy's wedding.

Tom and Kathleen Gilmour in a Montreal restaurant.

Charles and Antoinette Gundy at their wedding.

Beverley and Pauline Matthews.

Dorothy's husband Harold Crang and their son Rickey riding to hounds.

Harold Ritchie purchasing the J.C. Eno company.

Richie's 70-acre estate on Lake Simcoe, featuring seventeen bedrooms and tennis courts.

Ritchie bought his grand home at 40 Burton Road in Forest Hill Village in 1916.

CHAPTER FOUR

From Selling to Buying

By the early 1920s, Harold had gone about as far as he could with sales, but he still wanted to expand. The logical way to do so was to acquire some of the manufacturing companies for which he was selling goods. He had the advantage of knowing the market for those products better than anyone. He could assess the potential of the company and know where to expand the business. He already had his sales network in place.

"It was always our idea to acquire certain businesses," Harold said, "and from time to time we have been interested in enterprises—wholesale grocery houses, wholesale hardware houses etc. We have bought into them and we have sold out. We have always made money out of these enterprises, but at the end of the war, we ran into a bad loss."

The bad loss came from the lucrative chocolate market. Harold had been selling an enormous amount of chocolate in England, but some of the chocolate firms were in trouble, and Harold couldn't fill all the orders he had. "We found that we could not depend on these companies, so we started a chocolate factory. For a while, while export orders were coming in, this was satisfactory, but later we closed it with considerable loss. This was one business it did not pay us to continue. As we said then, we had nerve enough to start it so we had nerve enough to close it."

This may have been the Lorraine Chocolate Corporation, which listed Ruthven Hay, Harold's brother-in-law, as its treasurer. Ruthven was taking on more responsibilities in Harold's companies, and as Harold's empire expanded, so did Ruthven's role. Harold liked to employ people to whom he had some connection, so that his companies were a version of his family. By 1925, Glenn Robinson was listed as secretary of HFR Co. Both Ruthven and Glenn would rise through the corporate ranks.

The leap from representing companies to owning them required capital. Harold formed new firms, which were controlled by his holding company, International Proprietaries Ltd. It had only a handful of shareholders and was controlled by Harold.

"International Proprietaries Ltd is one of the best that has ever been offered to the Canadian public," Harold said. "We said that the first year we hoped to earn $825,000. We earned $1,114,000. The second year we said to the people to whom we had put out the issue that we hoped to make $900,000. We earned over $1,250,000. The entire control of International Proprietaries Ltd is in our hands. The control of the Ritchie companies is entirely in our hands. In fact, there are not any stockholders outside of the directors actively engaged in the Ritchie companies, and it might be interesting to say that the earnings of these companies, absolutely controlled here at 10 McCaul Street, are far in excess of some of our large Canadian banks. There is possibly not another business which is run more quietly or behind doors than this business."

This was certainly true. Harold's unassuming office and absentee profile in Toronto made him almost invisible. He had acquired significant wealth and a grand residence, but he was largely out of the public eye. He rarely gave interviews, and in those he did give, he often wanted his name left out. He does not appear to have socialized much. He was a 32nd degree Mason, a suitably secretive organization. Their stated mandate was, "32nd Degree Scottish Rite Freemasonry is a tight-knit community of Masons who seek to be the best version of themselves, find a deeper sense of purpose, and be of service to the world and our fellow man."

In addition to the Masons, Harold also belonged to the Royal Canadian Yacht Club, and the New York Athletic Club, which counted Vanderbilts and Roosevelts among its members (it was largely a yachting club then, and Harold had always been interested in boats). He belonged to other organizations as well: the Ontario Club, the American Club of London, the Canadian Club in New York. He would visit these when in the appropriate city. But for such a relentlessly social man, he appeared not to socialize much outside of work.

Harold was filled with these contradictions: he loved Canada and Toronto, but spent little time in either; he was a dedicated family man, yet was rarely at home; he had come from modest means and made more money than almost all of the Toronto establishment, but didn't appear to have any interest in becoming part of that group. This aloofness seems to have been the case in the US and England as well. He had no interest in social climbing or even acceptance in those milieus.

Harold had arrived in the big city as a provincial and may have remained one in the eyes of some of the city's business leaders. Yet many of those leaders were provincial in their enterprises, concentrating on the growing Canadian market. Harold was as internationalist as they came.

***

Throughout the 1920s, Harold had been buying small companies, keeping some, flipping others, and he'd had some success, but in 1928, he bought the company that would take him to another level. "In April 1928, word reached me that the firm of J. C. Eno

Limited might be sold," Harold said. "We had represented the Eno company from 1907. Our business had grown with them from Canada to over half the world." Harold went to London in June to negotiate the deal. "I went to England, negotiated the purchase, which took the best part of ten million dollars, and we bought that business after having plenty of competition." Because of Harold's contribution to the company's success, he had been given the opportunity to bid first. Harold bought Eno through his company International Proprietaries Ltd. Ten million dollars was an enormous sum at the time; Maple Leaf Gardens had been built at a cost of $1.5 million.

Eno's signature product and its biggest seller, Eno's Fruit Salts, had been created in 1861 by James Crossley in Newcastle. It was an antacid—a combination of sodium bicarbonate, tartaric acid and citric acid—that helped indigestion, although in the early years of patent medicine, it made bolder claims. In 1883, it had been advertised as a cure for cholera. By 1892, that claim had been reduced to "keeping the blood pure and free from disease."

The Eno purchase represented a new magnitude of capital expenditure for Harold, as well as a new direction. Like Warren Buffett years later, he researched successful companies (mostly by selling their products), assessed their worth, and then bought the company. They would include Thermogene, Virol, and Scott's Emulsion, among others. Increasingly, Harold turned his attention to patent medicines.

Patent medicines were a broad category that included many products that had little or no medicinal value. Some made you feel better, although this was largely because they contained alcohol, cannabis, opium, or cocaine. Some made you feel worse. Others were harmless. And some actually did at least part of what they claimed to do. Few of them were, in fact, patented, although their recipes were a secret.

Folk cures are as old as mankind, but patent medicines as Harold Ritchie knew them emerged in the early seventeenth century. In 1630, Anderson's Pills were introduced in England as a cure for a dozen maladies. Whether effective or fraudulent, patent medicines shared two essential traits: they were cheap to manufacture, and they relied heavily on salesmanship and advertising. Benjamin Brandreth's Vegetable Universal Pill became one of the best-selling patent medicines in America. In 1862, Brandreth's income was $600,000 (more than $9 million in today's currency). His pills were sold as purgatives that cleaned toxins from the blood but were pure quackery. He was, however, one of the largest buyers of advertising in the country; everyone knew the name of his product. And familiarity, as advertisers would soon realize, trumped authenticity and results. A few newspapers and almanacs sprung up solely to advertise a product: in Maine, the periodical *Comfort* was created to promote Oxien, made from the fruit of a baobab tree. The travelling medicine show, with its mythic snake oil salesman, was used by smaller manufacturers to get the word out. Then, as now, everyone wanted to feel better.

Then, even more than now, there were a host of diseases that had no real cure, and patent medicines offered hope, at least, if not an actual cure. Bonnore's Electro Magnetic Bathing Fluid allegedly cured cholera, epilepsy, and "female complaints." Many of the medicines were essentially placebos; others were narcotic and potentially addictive, and some, like Radithor, which was water laced with radium, and was radioactive, were occasionally fatal. William Radam's Microbe Killer came with the lofty claim, "Cures All Diseases." Ebenezer Sibly's Solar Tincture went a step further, claiming to "restore life in the event of sudden death."

No one rose from the dead, but consumers often felt uplifted by these cures, no doubt due to the grain alcohol, cocaine, and opium they contained. The downside of reliance on these ingredients—addiction, alcoholism, and death—eventually became apparent. In 1905, *Collier's Weekly* published a piece entitled, "The Great American Fraud," which looked at the dangers of some of the most famous patent medicines, and at how fraudulent and lucrative this unregulated industry had become. Newspapers followed up with their own investigations (although sometimes reluctantly, as patent medicines were among the largest advertising groups in the country). The *Collier's* piece was a factor in the passage of the Pure Food and Drug Act the following year. The act didn't initially ban addictive, potentially dangerous ingredients in medicines, but for the first time, manufacturers had to list the ingredients on the label.

Coca-Cola contained cocaine and was originally marketed as a cure for the curious trio of morphine addiction, indigestion, and impotence. Its owners eventually took the cocaine out of the product, which survived and then flourished as a soft drink. There is a rumour that Harold took the train to Atlanta with the idea of buying Coca-Cola, but ultimately declined. If true, it was one of Harold's few missteps.

Another medicine, "Bib-Label Lithiated Lemon-Lime Soda," contained lithium citrate, an anti-depressant. Its makers would not take the lithium out of the recipe until 1948, when they changed its name to 7Up.

Yet another popular soft drink began as a patent medicine. Hires Root Beer originally claimed that it could "purify the blood," before settling into a long, successful life simply as a soda fountain stalwart.

Beecham's Pills, initially a cure-all, then a laxative, were advertised as being made of medicinal herbs, which was partly true: it was made from aloe, ginger, and soap.

Dalby's Carminative was marketed as a way to soothe babies, which it did quite effectively, and not surprisingly given that its active ingredient was opium.

Godfrey's Cordial, marketed as "Mother's Friend," also used opium to soothe infants. There is an ad that features an illustration of two children, aged five or so, accompanied by the script: "Cocaine Toothache Drops: Instantaneous Cure! 15 cents."

Among the outlandish-sounding products that actually worked were Dr. Williams' Pink Pills for Pale People. They contained iron and were effective in treating anemia and chlorosis. Among the products that did nothing at all was Mrs. Moffat's Shoo-Fly Powders for Drunkenness.

The growth of the patent medicine industry was enabled both by the natural evolution of science, to the extent that it informed the creation of new products, and the industrial revolution, which transformed the way goods were produced. Thomas Beecham, who had begun his career as a travelling salesman in England, built the world's first factory for creating patent medicine in 1859.

Patent medicines got a big boost from the American Civil War (1861-1865), the nation's bloodiest (620,000 dead versus 405,399 lost in the Second World War). With all the carnage, there was an urgent need for medicines. A former Union cavalry commander named Eli Lilly set up a pharmaceutical business in 1876 in Indianapolis. One of his early innovations was a gelatin coating for pills and capsules. His first product was Succus Alteran, which was marketed as a "blood purifier." This was a common claim, perfectly suited for patent medicine: it sounded good and was impossible to disprove. And like many patent medicines, Succus Alteran also claimed to cure other, largely unrelated maladies—in this case syphilis, rheumatism, and eczema.

Legislators and regulators would slowly catch up with the patent medicine business, forcing products to either prove their claims for improved health, or drop them. Yet it was from these hopeful, slightly fraudulent beginnings that the pharmaceutical industry was born. A breakthrough came with Bayer, a German dye maker that had moved into patent medicines. Near the end of the nineteenth century, it was the first to commercialize aspirin, soon to become the most successful drug in history. The companies that formed to manufacture and market patent medicines tended not to specialize, selling drugs, cod liver oil, toothpaste, and hair gel, as well as medicine.

Harold, too, liked diversity. His companies were selling everything from hardware to brushes to groceries to salt water taffy, but patent medicines were made for him. He understood their unique potential. Eno's Fruit Salts no longer claimed to cure cholera, but it was an effective antacid and remains in production today as Eno, owned by pharmaceutical giant GlaxoSmithKline. Harold probably knew the company better than its chairman when he bought Eno on June 30, 1928.

Less than a week later, Harold was at a lavish celebration of the Eno company's Diamond Jubilee, a dinner held at London's luxurious Savoy Hotel. The event would have been planned months earlier and probably hadn't anticipated this change in ownership. Among the 250 guests were aristocrats, lords, members of parliament, the colonial secretary, and British captains of industry. They ate *Madrilene Froid en Tasse* and *Mignon d'Agneau Prince de Galles* and drank Mumm Cordon Rouge champagne and Heidsieck Dry Monopole champagne. They toasted the King, the empire, and trade, and drank liqueurs and smoked cigars. A large map showed all the countries where Eno's Fruit Salts were sold. All of London's press were there—*The Daily Chronicle, Daily Express, Daily Mail, Daily News, Daily Sketch, Daily Telegraph, Reuters, The Morning Post,* and the *Times*. As the owner of the company, Harold was ostensibly at the centre of this celebration. However, true to his nature, he appeared to find a place on the periphery.

The Right Honourable Sir Robert Horne gave a speech about the glory of the empire and its vast commercial reach. "It has grown in the way British things grow," he said, "but to a Frenchman it is completely incomprehensible. To him it is the most illogical thing in the world today." The irony perhaps lost on Sir Robert that the entire menu was in French and the champagnes they were toasting the empire with came from France. And there was the larger irony that the glorious British company they had all gathered to celebrate had been bought only days earlier by a colonial who had been born in a small village in a distant dominion.

Horne emphasized that trade with its own colonies was the prize. There was no need to cater to difficult European markets or explore distant South American countries. This was the opposite of Harold's philosophy, who was moving around the globe looking for opportunities, and who had expanded Eno's international profile.

While Horne and others spoke of the glories of England, the subtext of their speeches was, in fact, the decline of the Empire. Two years earlier, an imperial conference had finally defined the constitutional status of the dominions, and it was established that they had the right to full self-government and would no longer be required to follow British foreign policy, which meant they would no longer have to follow Britain into war. Politically, Britain was losing its grip on its empire, and it was losing its economic hegemony as well.

Britain had recently gone from a creditor nation to a debtor nation, borrowing heavily from the US to finance the First World War. There were troubles in Ireland and India, and, looming on the horizon, the disturbing strength of Germany. At home, there were constitutional issues and labour strife. Disgruntled, unemployed citizens were holding "hunger marches" in London and protesting on the grounds of the parliament buildings. The depression that would envelop much of the world in little more than a year had already begun in Britain.

Horne's speech was filled with bravado, but there was also a sense of British hubris. "We live entirely on our trade and commerce," he said. He warned that the Americans were persistent and were invading the colonies, selling everything from hair cream to automobiles. Britain, according to Horne, had become complacent. It had held to the belief that British goods were fundamentally better and would always be in demand. But America had more energy, more salesmen, and was more innovative. The US tailored its products to the market. The empire, with its centuries of dominance, still expected the market to adapt to its products. "We in this country did not take the same troubles as our competitors in making articles which suited the dominion markets," Horne warned. "Unless we wake up on this matter, we should be very seriously prejudiced."

The Right Honourable L.S. Amery, secretary of state for the dominion and colonies, stood up and spoke enviously of the progress made by America. "The American salesman pushes his wares with rare determination," Amery warned, "with great brain power, but he is inspired all the time also by the thought that he is not only selling his goods but that he is selling America." Amery said that Britain had to start thinking along the same lines. "To think imperially," he said, "is the beginning of the successful revival of British business."

The evening was, in some ways, a perfect microcosm of the empire. It began in glory and self-congratulatory toasts, but devolved into creeping doubt and subtle warnings. They were celebrating a British success story that was no longer British-owned. Within months, Harold would expand the business dramatically, and go much farther afield than the empire. Perhaps, as he sat there, half-listening to the speeches, he was already making plans.

He would end up keeping the factory in London, England, then quickly built factories in Canada, France, Germany, Spain, the US, Brazil, Argentina, Mexico, Australia, South Africa, and Venezuela. The product would soon be sold in eighty-three countries and, just as critically, advertised in seventy-three of those countries.

If Harold had nothing to learn from the somewhat hidebound British merchants, there were places in the Right Honourable Amery's speech where Harold would have concurred. Amery, in fact, may have gotten this idea from Harold. He suggested that it wasn't enough to send out salesmen to the territory; the head of the company should go out himself and see what was happening. "Someone else," Amery told the assembled, "it is true, may get orders for him, but let him go out and get them himself. It is only when the head of a business goes out himself to another country that he can realize at a glance in what respect the goods he makes do not meet the local needs, and he goes back determined to see how he can set the matter right. No report from an agent ever leads to the same prompt and definite action as what you have seen for yourself if you are the head of a firm. Again, it is only the man at the top who can judge, not only of the present, but of the future possibilities of a market. . . . He establishes the sense of personal contact which is as vital in business as it is in politics, and in doing so he can sell, not only his goods, but Britain and the imperial idea in a way that no one else can sell it for him. (Applause)."

This is precisely what Harold had been doing for two decades—visiting every market, every territory, meeting every customer, although he wasn't selling Britain's imperial interest. He had travelled more than most of the men in the room combined. He could have delivered a speech on the insularity of British commerce and the need to expand beyond the empire.

Amery talked nostalgically about Eno. "The name Eno conjures up for me so many memories of childhood," he said. "I was brought up on Eno." He quoted an old, incredibly baroque, Eno ad: "Only Truth can give True Representation, Only Reality can be of real profit. The Secret of Success—Sterling Honesty of Purpose. Without it, life is a Sham. The Value of Eno's Fruit Salt cannot be told."

Amery said of J. C. Eno, the company's founder (and the same could be said of Harold), "He was one of the very first men to realise the great truth that civilized man lives not by bread alone but mostly on patent medicines (laughter). . . . I doubt very much whether in the whole history of British advertising, or world advertising, for that matter, whether there was a more original genius, a more skilful user of advertisement than J. C. Eno (Applause)."

Wrapping up his long speech, Amery said, "I do not know whether, technically speaking, Mr. Harold Ritchie of Toronto is one of our hosts tonight, but we all know the very great and important part he has taken in the development of this great business—(applause)—and the part he has taken in bringing the enterprise and vigour of the colonies to an old-established, solidly rooted British business, with the happiest results to the vitality and prosperity of that business, which if I may say so, is a practical and admirable illustration of the benefits to be derived by that greater cooperation between the dominions of the crown and the old country of which we have heard so much this evening."

Harold was last to speak. "Mr. Chairman, my Lords and Gentlemen—for an ordinary colonial to break in here after the speeches made upon empire trade would almost put me in the class of the boy that should be spanked and put to bed," he said. "I have had the privilege for some twenty-one years of helping to build empire trade." He recounted the story when he'd first come over to London and been rebuffed by Eno, then made the audacious offer to double their trade in Canada. There were a dozen men in the audience who owned companies that were represented by the Harold F. Ritchie company, and he acknowledged them. "These gentlemen gave me an opportunity of representing them in different parts of the empire, and other parts of the world, as, for instance, South America, Central America, the United States of America, Canada, Australia, New Zealand, China, the West Indies, and many other countries."

This may have been Harold's subtle way of presenting the idea that, while imperial trade was a wonderful and sustaining thing, the future lay elsewhere—in countries where English wasn't spoken.

He was gracious and politic about a colonial acquiring a staid British business. "One thing that I am extremely proud of," he said, "is that I am able to come here at the diamond jubilee, the hundredth anniversary of Mr. Eno's birth, my own twenty-first birthday connection with the business, and to have the chairman, Colonel Allirusen, continue as the chairman of the company; the directors continue as directors; it is to me, a colonial, a former servant of the company, a very great honour and satisfaction."

There was great applause. Harold would likely have enjoyed a cigar and talked with some of the men about sales and markets and empire. Then he would have gone up to his hotel room, with his own pillow on the bed. Perhaps he stared out his window to the lights dimmed by London fog. This gray town and its history and traditions that had given the world so much, but now found itself in a world it no longer comprehended, and was somehow surprised.

Three months after the grand evening celebrating Eno, Harold bought another British company, Thermogene Company Limited, and its US subsidiary, Genotherm. Thermogene produced medical wadding that created heat and was used to combat bronchitis and other ailments. Both Eno and Thermogene were bought by International Proprietaries Ltd. The purchase wasn't just a change in scale, but of complexity. International Proprietaries, a public company owned by a handful of directors and controlled by Harold, was now at the top of a web of companies which it owned in whole or in part, and it gave every appearance of looking to increase its holdings.

In the first quarter after Harold's ownership, both Eno and Thermogene showed record profits. "Total sales for the first three months in 1929 throughout the entire world show a marked increase and operating overheads were no higher than in 1928," Harold reported.

Six months later, the stock market crashed. American banks failed. In 1930, the Smoot-Hawley Tariff Act was passed in the US, implementing protectionist tariffs on 20,000 different imported products. Countries around the world responded with their own tariffs and international trade suddenly got more expensive and more complicated. The tariff act was designed to help alleviate the dire economic toll of the depression but instead had the opposite effect. A petition signed by 1,028 economists was presented to American President Herbert Hoover, asking him to veto the legislation, and Henry Ford appealed to Hoover in person, calling it "economic stupidity." Hoover himself wasn't in favour of the tariffs, but he caved to pressure from his fellow Republicans, who felt the tariffs would preserve American jobs. They didn't. And they failed to preserve Hoover's Republican government; he was voted out of office in 1933.

Harold's response to the tariffs was to continue to open factories in foreign countries; what was produced there could be sold within the country without any tariffs applied. It also exposed his company to wildly fluctuating currencies and exchange rates, but while 1931 was a challenging year for most businesses and a catastrophic year for some, the Harold F. Ritchie Company reported healthy profits.

Harold continued to expand during the depression, a counterintuitive move, given the bleak economic outlook. "There is not a doubt that the business is going to continue to expand and grow," he said. "Last year (1930) was a long way the best year we ever had in business and while everybody is hollering hard times, we are marching straight on."

In 1931, Harold acquired the Browne and Scott Company, which sold Scott's Emulsion, which he had seen advertised in the Little Current newspaper as a child. Essentially cod liver oil, Scott's emulsion also contained glycerine, which sweetened the bitter taste. It was created in 1873 in New York by Alfred B. Scott, who noted the interest in cod liver oil as a health supplement. People bought into its health benefits but hated the taste. The emulsification process sweetened the taste, and his product was a hit. In 1889, it featured a morbid ad that had a young girl in bed, her mother beseeching a doctor, "Oh! Doctor, must my darling die?" The doctor responds, "There's very little hope, but try Scott's Emulsion." It was also said to cure tuberculosis. It didn't, but it was an extremely successful product, and Scott and Browne already had factories in Canada, England, Spain, Portugal, Italy, and France.

CARLOAD RITCHIE

By the time Harold bought the company, it had abandoned the idea that Scott's Emulsion cured tuberculosis. But it did claim to be four times easier to digest than regular cod liver oil. On the packaging was a vague guarantee: "We guarantee that Scott's Emulsion when assayed biologically contained sufficient Vitamin A and Vitamin D units to meet the daily dosage requirements . . ."

Harold expanded its global reach with his sales network and continued the aggressive marketing campaign, although his ads weren't as melodramatic as the nineteenth-century versions. It is still being sold today, in pill form, by GlaxoSmithKline. The pills come in bottles with happy cartoon figures on them, and the advertising concentrates on the Vitamin A and D it contains.

Harold sold other medicines and treatments, including Brown's Bronchial Troche, Brown's Vermifuge Comfits, Keating's Powder (for killing insects), Glaxo ("The Super Milk that Builds Bonnie Babies"), and Pluto Water, recommended by doctors as a cure for "intestinal stasis." Perhaps his most dubious product was Phosferene, which was advertised as "The Greatest of All Tonics, a proven remedy for: Influenza, Maternity Weakness, Lassitude, Sciatica, Premature Decay, Neuralgia, Headache, Malaria, Nervous Debility, and Sleeplessness." Remarkably, it is still being sold, as a vitamin now, and it claims to cure almost as many problems, albeit different ones: eye disorders, convulsions, pregnancy complications, and anemia, among them.

Another doubtful product was Fellows Compound Syrup of Hypophosphites. It was sold more to doctors than the general public, and like Phosferene, it claimed to cure a wide variety of illnesses. Unfortunately, it contained strychnine, a poison. Its creator, James Fellows, advertised it as "an excellent recuperative tonic" that could be effective against "anemia, neurasthenia, bronchitis, influenza, pulmonary tuberculosis, and wasting diseases of childhood, and during convalescence from exhausting diseases." The strychnine could produce convulsions in those who took it. Nevertheless, it was a great success and made Fellows a wealthy man. He died an invalid in 1889, his own tonic ineffective against his "exhausting disease."

A Toronto photograph from 1912 shows a billboard on the corner of Yonge and Shuter Streets advertising Bovril, "The Great Body Builder." It was something Harold would likely have seen. Perhaps he stared up at it and was inspired. He would eventually represent Bovril as a salesman.

Bovril had been developed by John Lawson Johnston, a Scot living in Canada, who had the job of supplying Napoleon III's troops with beef in 1870 during the Franco-Prussian War. Shipping beef from Canada and Argentina was expensive and presented the logistical problem of transporting live animals across the Atlantic. As an alternative, Johnston created a meat extract originally sold in bottles as a jelly, and later in cubes and granules. By adding hot water, a hearty, salty beef broth was created.

By 1888, it was sold throughout Great Britain, and gained increased popularity during the First World War as a "war food." All you had to do was add water and you had a healthy broth, or as some British termed it "beef tea." Bovril was one of the few products to use the Pope in its advertisements. A drawing of Pope Leo XIII seated on his throne holding a cup of Bovril had the line: "The Two Infallible Powers—The Pope & Bovril."

Another of Harold's companies was Virol, a product developed by Bovril and spun into a separate company. In an ad from 1927, there is a photograph of a naked child of about two. The pitch line is: "The World's Most Beautiful Child was given VIROL from birth." The product was added to milk as a supplement and contained refined beef fat, sugar, iron phosphate, and orange juice, among other ingredients. It was still being manufactured in the 1980s.

Harold was adept at picking products that had broad market appeal and the possibility of further growth. "We are constantly having new agencies offered to us," he said. "We are rather particular about what we take on."

He continued to focus heavily on patent medicines, and why not? They were inexpensive to produce, highly profitable, and a perfect fit with his sales network. All they needed was a good advertising campaign and his seasoned sales force would rack up orders. It was a formula that Big Pharma would later embrace.

"Our business is not confined to the drug business," Harold liked to point out. He was still in the grocery business, hardware, stationary, and toys. He sold Fralinger's salt water taffy, Sunset soap dyes, Gorham silver polish, A.1. sauce, Hyglo Manicure Products, among many others. But these were largely businesses for which he was a commissioned sales agent. What he bought was drug companies. They were the future.

CHAPTER FIVE

A Thing of Beauty

O**N MARCH 1, 1930,** Harold bought the Pompeian Company, which manufactured cosmetics. Up until this point, Harold had no real public profile. The purchase of Eno in 1928 had oddly brought very little public attention. But Pompeian caught the interest of the media. *The Telegram* did a lengthy profile, as did *The Canadian,* a prominent publication at the time ("A different and better magazine"). "The Odyssey of a Super-Salesman" was the title in *The Canadian,* June 1930. It described Harold as "a heavy-jowled man with personality stamped upon every feature." The article seized on the uniqueness of his commercial empire: "we do not think of our financiers and industrialists controlling big business in countries other than our own." Both the *Toronto Star* article and *The Canadian* profile also touched on the theme of Canadian nationalism. It was a delicate moment in the country's history, one where Canada was trying to define itself between the looming shadows of Great Britain and America. Harold had achieved success outside the country's borders, which gave him a gravitas that local success couldn't achieve. And he had steadfastly held to his Canadian identity. "Mr. Ritchie, as a Canadian, never pretends to be anything else," the profile stated. "He also always refers with pride, no matter where he is, to the fact that the head office of his organization is in Toronto. He is always speaking a good word for Toronto wherever he is."

With Pompeian, Harold now had a product that was international, recognizable and glamourous. Originally a face cream for men, applied after shaving, Pompeian was created by Cleveland pharmacist Fred Stecher in 1901 and marketed as Pompeian Massage Cream and Skin Food. By 1910, there was a version for women and it became the best-selling face cream in the US, aided by an aggressive advertising campaign that was budgeted at $250,000 in 1907. It contained benzaldehyde (artificial almond oil) and benzoic acid, a preservative, and claimed to clean better than any soap. "Get All the Dirt Out of Your Skin," the early ads read.

The success of the initial cream led to a dozen other products: Pompeian Hair Massage, day cream, beauty powder, lipstick, and perfume among others. In 1927, it was sold to Colgate

& Company. The following year, Colgate merged with the Palmolive-Peet Company and had sales of $2,122,255, with a profit of $570,382.

"We represented the Pompeian Company for years," Harold told the *Toronto Evening Telegram*, "and up until 1927 when this business was purchased by Colgate & Company, we handled the sales in Canada and some of the foreign territories. Naturally, the Colgate company had their own organization and wanted to handle their own sales. In 1928, the Colgate company merged with the Palmolive-Peet Company into a new organization known as Colgate-Palmolive-Peet Company. After this merger was completed, they discovered that there was a good deal of duplication. The Palmolive Company had competitive lines to the Pompeian Company. It meant dropping some of their own lines if they wanted to push the sale of Pompeian. It meant divided effort. After months of negotiations, we were able to acquire this business at a price we considered very advantageous." It was sold to Harold and partners for $1,375,000 (US), considerably less than its total sales in 1928, a bargain.

His partners were the Shoemaker family of Elmira, New York, which owned Frostilla, a hand cream. Frostilla was developed by a pharmacist named Clay Holmes in 1884, in Elmira, New York. Holmes' simple formula of glycerin, alcohol and quince seed became a big seller. He sold the company to James Monroe Shoemaker, but Holmes remained the marketing force behind it.

CARLOAD RITCHIE

He pioneered the idea of giving out free samples, which proved very effective and was quickly adopted by competitors (and remains a primary marketing tool for Big Pharma). Harold had acquired the rights to sell Frostilla around the world, so he and Shoemaker already had a partnership; they formed a consortium and bought Pompeian.

Harold planned an aggressive advertising campaign. "The Pompeian Company is one of the best-known cosmetic houses in the world," he said, "and with our distributing organization and with our ideas of general publicity we believe we will make this a greater company than it ever was. We have plans to buy other companies."

Harold was one of the few businessmen looking to buy companies in the early 1930s. The depression was taking a toll. Thirty percent of the Canadian labour force was unemployed. On the prairies, many of the towns Harold had visited thirty years earlier had been decimated by the dust bowl. Men rode the rails, going from city to city, looking for work. Soup kitchens couldn't handle the numbers that showed up each day. The Canadian government only had one economist, and he worked for the department of foreign affairs; it was understood that the economy would take care of itself. Prime Minister Mackenzie King, a dull, reliable man, at least in terms of policy, had called an election in 1930 after consulting a medium, who he often employed to talk to his dead mother and his dead dog, Pat. A closet spiritualist, King later expanded his network of dead friends to include Philip the Apostle, the Medici family, and Leonardo da Vinci. He lost to Conservative leader R. B. Bennett that year, but thought it might be a strategic loss. King realized that no one could do much about the depression and Bennett would bear the brunt of it, then be voted out.

Indeed, Prime Minister Richard Bedford Bennett's policies did little to mitigate the misery being felt across the country, and he spent his evenings in his Château Laurier suite answering desperate letters from Canadians asking for five dollars or a winter coat for their child. In Toronto, there were bread lines. The government would adopt strategies to keep unemployed men working, such as hiring them to plant trees, build roads, and work on the Royal Ontario Museum.

Despite the crash, or perhaps because of it, Harold continued his extensive travel schedule. In April 1930, he, Berta, Dorothy, and Kathleen sailed to Southampton and stayed on the continent for two months. Along with Harold was Ruthven Hay and John Spence, the secretary of the Harold F. Ritchie Company. The following year, Berta took all four of her daughters to Bermuda on a vacation. Harold was adept at combining family and business on these trips. In March 1932, he, Berta, and John Spence flew to South America, visiting Port of Spain, Trinidad; San Juan, Puerto Rico; and Miami before returning home. Later that year, as the economic crisis deepened, Harold would embark on the longest trip of his well-travelled life.

In August 1932, he set out on a 25,000-mile journey through Central and South America. It was reputed to be the longest voyage by air in the world at the time. They would begin with a trip to New York by train in the company of Charles Weedon, manager of the J.C. Eno Co, and Spence. There they would meet with Marius Bressoud of Scott & Browne, and the four of them would take another train to Miami and, from there, head further south, mostly by plane.

It was counter-intuitive to undertake this kind of journey when the world was engulfed by the depression, with protective tariffs being erected globally, and consumer spending at forbidding lows. The sales world was contracting. But, against the odds, Harold's commercial world was continuing to expand. "The business is there if we go after it," he told *The Globe* on the eve of his departure.

Harold felt that Canada had the banking network, the brains, and manufacturing expertise to go out into the world, but most companies left "other fellows" to develop their foreign business. "I do not think that is good business," he said. "To me, it is axiomatic that if you want to sell, you must let other people know what you have to sell. If they will not come to your door, you must go to their door. I am amazed at the number of men who are still wringing their hands, complaining that export trade is an impossibility." He wished they would join him in South America.

A THING OF BEAUTY

One of the reasons no one was going to South America was that it was affected by the depression even more than North America. In many Latin American and South American countries, there was political chaos as well as economic turmoil. The Brazilian Olympic team financed its trip to the Los Angeles Olympics that year by selling coffee along the way, a commodity that was worth a third of what it had been three years earlier (the team failed to medal).

From Miami, Harold and his entourage flew on Pan American airlines to Cuba, which had a brutal government and was on the brink of revolution. On top of that, the island was hit by a series of deadly earthquakes. "Our first jump was over almost before it began," Harold said. "It landed us in Cienfuegos, Cuba. From there, we went over the old Spanish Main to Kingston, Jamaica. We made Barranquilla in Colombia in one jump." He had already established a factory there for both Eno and Scott's Emulsion. Then it was on to Bogota. "We rose only 1,200 feet in the first thousand miles, and then in a few hours soared 9,800 feet and dropped over the rim of high mountains down to the enormous plateau on which stands the progressive city of Bogota." All of this was undertaken in the very early days of commercial air travel. American Airlines had only been founded in 1926 and very few people had flown among the clouds.

Bogota may have been progressive, but Colombia was at war with Peru at the time, battling over disputed territory in the Amazon basin. Harold was more concerned with the tariff barriers installed to battle those of the US. "If tariff barriers are erected against you," he said, "you must get in behind the tariff barriers. If you want to do business with a country, it is reasonable that you should do business inside its frontiers and contribute to its support. I think one of Great Britain's troubles is that it has too long tried to ship to the whole world instead of going out into the world and manufacturing. You cannot be an alien and transient everywhere. We are putting factories in South America. In addition to the one in Colombia, we have started them this year in Caracas, Venezuela, Rio de Janeiro, and Buenos Aires. Next year, we will have them in Lima, Peru, Montevideo, Uruguay, in Mexico City, and Havana."

Harold was a firm believer in viewing all markets first hand, gaining insight and an understanding of the people, the culture, and local trade laws. "Travelling gives you an insight into foreign markets which you could not possibly get by staying at home," he said. "You learn something of other people's psychology. You become, to an extent, one of them, and are better able to cater to their tastes. International trade will certainly keep on dwindling without international contacts. It is regrettable to me that I did not come across any Canadian businessmen travelling in South America. If we want trade there, we must go there."

Going there, however, was both expensive and complicated. Some of the planes that Harold flew in were Pan American aircraft, which had only begun operations in 1927, although for smaller centres, he had to charter private planes. It was luxurious, glamourous, and expensive: a trip of 12,000 miles could cost $20,000 in today's currency. A major reason few people had flown—in 1930, only 6,000 Americans had travelled by plane—was that few could afford it. And while luxurious, air travel was not especially fast: between 140 and 200 miles per hour. Not for nothing were the Pan American planes still called flying boats (one of its primary aircraft was the Sikorsky S-38 Flying Boat). The planes also needed to stop frequently for refueling. A 25,000 mile trip involved more than a dozen flights, a daunting total given the dangers inherent in take-offs and landings.

From Colombia, Harold flew to Venezuela, where he visited Maracaibo, La Guara, and Caracas. Venezuela had a small population, mostly poor and illiterate, but the discovery of oil in 1922 was re-shaping the country, and Harold saw possibilities for sales. "It has no external debt," he observed, "it is ruled efficiently by a dictator and has splendid roads and schools and a very small business tax."

Wherever he went, he looked for opportunities. He made a note of what others were selling and what no one else was selling. He saw possibilities for Canadian butter. "In those hot countries, all butter is in tins. I saw New Zealand and Danish tins everywhere, but not Canadian tins. We could build up a big export trade for our butter down there."

From Venezuela, Harold first went to Trinidad, then to British Guyana. The plane flew over the infamous Devil's Island penal colony, then on to Para, Brazil, the rubber port. He stopped in Fortaleza, Natal, Pernambuco, Maceio, and Bahia. "Brazil," Harold said, "is, of course, colossal in size, as large as Canada and more full of potential than any other South American country. On account of revolutionary disturbances, we were unable to go into the port of Santos or into Sao Paulo." The Paulista War in the state of Sao Paulo was a revolt against the 1930 coup d'état. At the time, South America was a patchwork of revolutions, juntas, dictators, and economic strife, but Harold remained sanguine. "We covered the coast pretty thoroughly," he said, "and there was scarcely a town we visited in which there is not a good outlet for Canadian products."

Harold's days of selling on the Canadian prairies and in northern Ontario had taught him not to neglect the smaller centres. They were often overlooked by other salespeople and those orders added up. "Brazil wants our products," he said, "and it has many products of its own which we can use. It is the greatest coffee country in the world, the greatest rubber country. And we are a favoured nation there. It is one of the greatest markets for Canadian dried fish and also for canned goods, biscuits, and proprietaries of all kinds. Our Eno factory is doing well and we look forward to a very great development, especially when exchange difficulties are ironed out."

Before leaving Brazil, he made a stop at Porto Alegre. "Once it was only a name to me," Harold said. "Now I know it is a city of great importance and a thriving shipping centre. There is a big German settlement there and the place has a future."

Argentina, Harold felt, was one of the great countries in the world, and had a bright future. It had experienced a military coup in 1930, and thousands of anarchists and communists had been executed. Things remained tense, politically, with underground movements threatening to erupt. But its beef trade was relatively unaffected.

Crossing the Andes reminded Harold of the Rockies. "Mendoza, the last stop prior to the jump over the Andes to Santiago, in Chile, is like an enlarged Calgary. And the towns you see en route might be Portage la Prairie, Brandon, Moose Jaw, or Medicine Hat. The Andes are certainly impressive, but they furnish a spectacle of lonely bleakness which is difficult to forget. We went up 22,000 feet, close to the famous Cap de Aconcagua, which is 23,000 feet." Passengers were given oxygen tanks, although Harold didn't use his. It was a dizzying descent down into Santiago. They took a train to Valparaiso, but used a car for the return. "That was the wildest motor ride I have ever had," Harold said. "On one mountain that has forty-eight hairpin curves, we got lost in the clouds and we never could tell when we were going to take a bigger drop than that over Niagara Falls. I believe that in the mountains, the plane is safer."

Chilean president Carlos Ibáñez del Campo had resigned and the country was in a state of economic and political chaos. "The government was changing about as regularly as wash day," Harold observed, "but nonetheless, Chile was quiet."

While flying along the mountainous coast of Chile, Harold asked the pilot what he would do if he had to make an emergency landing. His reply was, "We are up 10,000 feet so if the engine failed I would have some time to look around. I would not look for a level patch—there is no such thing—but I would try to spot a wedge-shaped valley. You see, if I got into that, the plane would not roll over sideways. I have had two such landings, and smashed two planes, but I'm still alive, and I never lost a passenger."

The adoption of standardized cabin pressurization didn't arrive until the 1940s, hence the passengers' reliance on oxygen tanks when flying over mountains. Air turbulence was a much bigger factor; planes could drop hundreds of feet without warning. Despite its pitfalls, air travel was still the fastest way to get around, and Harold was keen to cover as much ground as possible. "Air service is amazingly efficient," he said.

In addition to buying and selling opportunities, Harold gained a detailed sense of what powered the various South American economies. "From Antofagasta," he said, "the first stop north of Santiago, you are in the nitrate country. The deposits which come from the decayed vegetation of the tropical age are placed in tanks of water and the nitrates float to the top. Fortunes were made out of these deposits, but not now. The market is gone. Cattle and copper, two other of Chile's chief products, are also a drag on the market, so the country at present is in a bad way."

In Peru, now travelling by seaplanes, Harold saw hundreds of miles of oil fields. "Lima is a really modern, beautiful city with splendid hotels and fine stores," he observed, "but underneath all Lima's beauty is the ugliness of economic adversity. It doesn't suffer as Chile does, but it is far from economic health."

It was a full day's flight north to Guayaquil, Ecuador. Ecuador's cacao exports had dried up after the crash, and the country had experienced a military coup a year earlier, and was now on the brink of civil war, but Harold concentrated on the markets. "We received a warm welcome from the people of Guayaquil," Harold said, "but also from the insects. But the Guayaquil insects are nothing compared to those of Santa Elena, a hundred miles distant on a sand point reaching far out into the ocean. It is the central cable station for South America. I do not advise you to visit Santa Elena unless you have a skin like a rhinoceros or a hard-shelled crab. The Santa Elena insects do not like northerners. But it is worthwhile going to Ecuador. It is a market well worth cultivating."

From Ecuador, it was another day's flying to Panama, which had experienced a revolt the year before and the government remained fragile. In nearby El Salvador, the government massacred more than 10,000 peasants who rose up against the authorities. The entire region was given to political instability at the best of times, and the depression had added further pressures on the Central and South American economies.

Harold may have been the only North American salesman on the continent at the time. It gave him a distinct advantage, although he was prepared to share his knowledge of the territories. "In these days," Harold said, "we need, above all other things, to pool trade data. It is just enlightened self-interest. Your own prosperity is greater if your neighbours are prosperous."

To get home, there was a long flight to Kingston, Jamaica, then another to Miami. Harold and his entourage took a train to Jacksonville, then flew to Newark, and took the train from New York to Toronto. They had been gone six weeks. The journey was expensive, and the logistics would have been almost overwhelming at the time, but Harold said he had accomplished in six weeks what would have previously taken six months if he'd gone by boat and train. Air travel was actually an economy, he reasoned, and it was the way of the future. "I do not hesitate to say that the plane is the coming method of transportation for modern business."

On his lengthy trip, Harold had encountered dictators, inequality, tariffs, poverty, language barriers, and insects (though growing up in Little Current he would have been conversant with black flies and mosquitos). There was a revolution in the state of Sao Paulo, where the people had risen up against President Getulio Vargas. In Havana, the Cuban people had a violent revolt against President Gerardo Machado's attempt to become president-for-life. There were good reasons he hadn't seen any other sales people on his travels. Yet he found opportunity and markets. He was nothing if not an optimist.

* * *

In the early winter of 1932, Harold received the news that his mother had died. Matilda Jane Ritchie passed on December 29, at the age of seventy-nine. She had been down with the flu, and it had turned into pneumonia. It was hoped that she would rally, but she finally succumbed. Harold, his sister Lavinia and brother Morland, were all at her bedside when she died. Harold had been close to his mother. They looked alike, and at the United Church in Little Current, he eulogized her as "the best mother a man could have."

In 1933, the nadir of the depression, the Harold F. Ritchie companies reported that the sum total of their business was flat. "In South Africa we will have a large increase in business, a large increase in the United States and other countries," Harold told *The Globe*, "against decreases in some of the countries. All in all, the business will be practically the same as last year. We may even be a little ahead."

This was anomalous, and a real accomplishment given the circumstances. Bankruptcies abounded. Banks and businesses were failing in droves. Building permits dropped in the cities; almost no one was building anything. In Winnipeg, 44,000 people were on relief. In Toronto, the figure was much higher. Bad times brought social unrest, and politics were in turmoil. Prime Minister Bennett was in the difficult position of worrying about the spread of both communism and fascism. In 1933, anti-Semitic violence broke out in Toronto's Christie Pits, where a Jewish baseball team was playing. There were 10,000 spectators, among them, members of the Swastika Club yelling "Heil Hitler!" The fighting lasted for six hours, in part because police were monitoring a communist meeting in another part of town. Communist leaders were not being monitored but arrested in other parts of the country. The prairies that Harold had once covered were now devastated by drought. The collapsing economy called for desperate measures. In Alberta, Premier William "Bible Bill" Aberhart, who hosted a radio bible show, wanted the province to print its own money. "The spirit of Christ has gripped me," he said.

And yet Harold's empire rolled along. The *Ottawa Journal* noted, "Distinct improvement in the patent medicine business throughout the empire was reported today by Harold F. Ritchie of Toronto, president of International Proprietaries Ltd., which has manufacturing establishments in 94 countries." Harold was quoted in the article. "There has been no depression as far as these companies are concerned," he said. "We have had no lay-offs. On the contrary, we have added to our staff. I am confident that with the signing of the empire trade pact, Canada has turned the corner of prosperity. Business in '32 was better than '31."

Having thoroughly covered both the Americas, Harold now planned to turn his attention to Africa. He had already established an operation in Cape Town, and South African profits were up. His plan was to fly down the western coast of Africa and look for business there. He would end the trip in Cape Town. Berta could accompany him and return to the scene of her teaching efforts. But the Africa trip never happened.

CHAPTER SIX

Woodlands

IN AUGUST 1930, Harold bought Woodlands, an estate on the north shore of Kempenfelt Bay, part of Lake Simcoe, located about seven kilometres east of Barrie, Ontario. The main house had been built in 1870 by Richard Power, an Irish immigrant who had been in the lumber business in Ireland. It came with seventy acres, 2,500 feet of lake frontage, a putting green, tennis courts, and seventeen bedrooms. It was the grandest property in the area.

The land that Woodlands is on was originally intended for Black settlers who received land in return for military service. In 1828, William Davenport received 100 acres on what was then called Wilberforce Street, named for William Wilberforce, a British parliamentarian who lobbied against slavery. Davenport sold the land after two years, and it changed hands a few times before Power bought it in 1869.

Power spent an estimated $30,000 to build Woodlands, at a time when houses sold for less than $1,000. It was essentially a duplicate of a manor house in Ireland that belonged to his family. Power was described by a fellow Irishman as a "gentleman who brings his culture and his money to increase our wealth and make Canada morally and socially more attractive." Whatever his social and moral contribution, Power suffered financial setbacks and in 1886 he sold Woodlands to Dugald Crawford, a St. Louis merchant. Crawford spent $50,000 landscaping and improving Woodlands, but by 1905, he was bankrupt and Woodlands became the property of the Girard National Bank of Philadelphia. The bank, in turn, sold the estate to a Philadelphia man who flipped it immediately to Lieutenant-Colonel Frederic Nicholls of Toronto for $10,500. Two years later, Nicholls sold Woodlands for $11,500 to Arthur Peuchen.

Peuchen was the president of the Standard Chemical Company, part of Toronto's staid business establishment. He was fifty-two when he had the bad luck to board the *Titanic* on April 10, 1912. It could be argued that it was even worse luck that he survived the disaster. A major in the Queen's Own Rifles and a yachtsman, Peuchen was dismayed to find that the Titanic's captain was Edward John Smith, who had had earlier mishaps at sea. When the ship hit the fateful iceberg, Peuchen went to inspect the damage personally. There was ice inside the railing at the bow. He returned to his cabin and put on heavy clothing and his life preserver. He left behind more than $200,000 in investments and instead took his lucky pearl pin and three oranges.

There are a few versions of what happened next. Peuchen said that, as an experienced sailor, he was told he was needed on the lifeboats, which, as the law of the sea had it, were boarded with women and children first. Second officer D.C.H. Lightoller was in lifeboat No. 6 and asked Peuchen to help. Peuchen insisted on a note saying that he was ordered off the *Titanic*. Lightoller complied, writing, "Major Peuchen was ordered into the boat by me, owing to the fact that I required a seaman, which he proved to be, as well as a brave man." There were only twenty passengers in a boat that held sixty. Peuchen survived, while 1,517 people, mostly men, died.

When Peuchen got back to Toronto, the newspapers ostracized him. "He said he was a yachtsman. If it had been a fire, he would have said he was a fireman," one account read. His family was jeered on the street and his children received hate mail. Differing versions of his experience emerged, and the version that hardened in the public imagination said that he was a coward. It didn't help that one of the women in his lifeboat, Margaret "Molly" Brown, an American socialite, accused him of slacking off as an oarsman. The "Unsinkable Molly Brown," as she would be called, claimed she wanted to steer the boat back to the debris and pick up survivors but was overruled by Robert Hichens, the quartermaster, who was worried they would be caught in the suction of the sinking ship. Brown was immortalized in a Broadway musical, and later in a film titled *The Unsinkable Molly Brown*. Her account had a whiff of self-mythology. Peuchen's story continued to be dogged by troubling questions: why did they need another experienced seaman with two already on board?

How much truth there was in either Brown's or Peuchen's account soon ceased to matter: myth was taking over, a more potent force than history. Peuchen's social status in Toronto was shaken and he spent the First World War in London, commanding the Home Battalion of the Queen's Own Rifles. When he returned to Canada, the *Titanic* stigma remained. His nephew said, "the backlash of the *Titanic* played havoc with my uncle's enterprises . . . years after, when I would mention my uncle, people would say, 'oh yes, he's the man who dressed in woman's clothes to get off the *Titanic*.'" In the 1920s, some of Peuchen's business ventures failed, and when he died in 1929, his considerable wealth was drastically diminished. (In 1987, a Titanic salvage team found Peuchen's wallet, containing his business card and streetcar tickets.)

After Peuchen's death, there was a plan to convert Woodlands into a hotel. Central Ontario Hotels planned to buy it and open a year-round resort that they would name the Kempenfelt Inn for the bay it fronted. Instead, the administrators of Peuchen's estate sold Woodlands to Harold Ritchie for $30,000, exactly what it had cost Richard Powers to build sixty years earlier.

Woodlands' architecture is Gothic Revival, the dominant style around the time of confederation. It's seen in the older buildings on the University of Toronto campus, and it was a style favoured by wealthy Ontarians. Inside the main entrance was a grand staircase that ascended toward a sixty-foot dome. There were seventeen bedrooms, a billiard room, horse stables, a boathouse and two beaches—one facing the morning sun, the other facing the afternoon sun. There was a greenhouse and a water wheel and an extensive verandah facing the water. The high ceilings had elaborate crown molding imported from Ireland. It had been a complex structure to build, requiring skilled craftsmen. Woodlands was more estate than summer home and it came with a history of bankruptcy and scandal, but it was refuge, both from the humid Toronto summers and the predations of the depression. As a sales agent for groceries and staples that people had to buy whatever their economic circumstances, and for patent medicines that thrived in times of suffering, Harold was singularly shielded against the turmoil of the depression, and Woodlands was his idyllic oasis.

CHAPTER SEVEN

Carload's Legacy

HAROLD DIDN'T LIVE TO travel to Africa, or to see his patent medicines evolve into Big Pharma. He died at ten minutes to noon on February 22, 1933, at the Toronto General Hospital. He had turned fifty-two only two days earlier. It is fitting that such an elusive man would have several different announced causes of death: appendicitis, overwork, and cardiac and respiratory failure during gallbladder surgery. The last cause is the most likely. He had been in the hospital for a few days, but his death was a shock to his family.

A service was held at his home at 40 Burton Road on February 25, presided over by the Reverend W. E. Wilson, a pastor at the King Street United Church who had known Harold from Manitoulin. It was a private ceremony, although hundreds came to pay their respects. Harold's father was too ill to make the journey from Manitoulin. His son's casket was in the great room of the house, covered in roses. "As a son of Canada," Reverend Wilson said, "Harold F. Ritchie is certainly one of whom Canada may be proud. He was a big man in every way, and yet in my associations with him, I found him very humble. He was always doing good turns for his friends and acquaintances, without letting anyone know about them. Although a great man, and a rich man, he never forgot his friends of boyhood days or of any other day."

The clergyman recalled that when Harold returned to Manitoulin to visit his parents, he would look up old friends as well, some of whom he hired to work in his company. "He was, in all things," Reverend Wilson said, "his mother's son."

The casket was borne out of the house by Tom Gilmour, A. Hambly, Ian Dowie, Donald Farquharson, John Spence, Harold Crang, William Wilson, and Cameron McKenzie. One of the honourary pallbearers was Senator Arthur Meighen, who had been the ninth prime minister of Canada.

Harold was taken to the Mount Pleasant Cemetery that day. On December 13, ten months after his death, he was lowered into a plot within its gates that had been purchased by Berta, and finally laid to rest.

On March 2, *The Expositor* newspaper in Little Current ran a lengthy obituary that had appeared in a Toronto daily. On the next page was an ad for W. D. Ritchie & Son ("real values and real service: fancy seedless raisins, 2 lbs 25 cents; Super Suds, 2 pkgs. 25 cents; Bacon, sugar cured, 17 cents per Lb.").

* * *

In his eulogy for Harold, Reverend Wilson had said, "Death does not destroy personality. His personality and his works will live after him."

This was only partly true. It was Harold's energy and personality that had built his companies and had kept them expanding, even in hard times. He had gone to every territory, met with every client. He had established a strong management team, but it was his unique will and energy that sustained his vast operation.

Berta had been vice-president of the Harold F. Ritchie Company, and chairman of International Proprietaries Co., one of the few female executives at the time. Two months after Harold died, she became president of Harold F. Ritchie Co. Within a year of Harold's death, she sold International Proprietaries Co. to the London & Yorkshire Trust in London, England, for 2.5 million pounds, reported in Canada as $12,425,000. International Proprietaries was essentially a holding company for Eno, and it also controlled Thermogene, which was part of the deal. Also included in the transaction were controlling shares in all three of the Harold F. Ritchie companies: the Canadian, American, and UK versions. Berta said the reason for the sale was that she wanted to pursue "private interests," most likely her philanthropic work.

But she knew that it was Harold who was responsible for the companies' ongoing success. In many ways, Harold was his empire. And in the middle of a depression with no end in sight, it was possible, even likely, that the worth of the companies would diminish without Harold's animating energy. Selling the company made sense, if she could find a buyer. As it was, she sold at a good price in a difficult market. The appeal for the British trust company was partly the extensive sales and distribution network that Harold had built, still the largest in the world. But there was another, perhaps more important reason. In the coverage of the deal in British newspapers, there was a note of triumph that Eno had been "repatriated." After five years, it had been brought back to British soil. It was viewed as a national treasure, albeit one that owed its recent success to its Canadian owner, the person who had engineered Eno's global expansion.

Harold's father, William, died in July 1934 at the age of seventy-nine at Simcoe Hall, in Allandale (not far from Woodlands), and was buried in the Mountain View Cemetery in Little Current, beside Matilda. Berta's father, Archibald, died a month later and was buried in the New Hope Cemetery in Hespeler. He had been living with Berta on Burton Road since 1921, and in August, he died of "senility with uraemia," which likely meant kidney failure.

He was eighty-nine. Berta lost her husband, her father, and her father-in-law within eighteen months of one another.

Berta received life insurance totaling $170,314.01, and Harold's will stipulated that she would receive another $50,000 a year, while each daughter would receive $10,000 per annum. Berta also received the residences and the cars. Other relatives and household servants received annuities of up to $5,000 per year.

On May 8, 1935, two years after Harold's death, a *Globe* headline blared, "$800,000 Bill for Ritchie Estate." Ontario Premier Mitchell Hepburn made the announcement at Queen's Park, claiming that the Ritchie estate had been undervalued by $2,000,000. Hepburn was reviewing 100 estates, and said, "we are going to collect all that is coming to us."

Hepburn, the Liberal premier, was an affable, hard-drinking womanizer who lived in a suite in the King Edward Hotel, and travelled with his bodyguard/bartender and a handful of female escorts who called him "Chief." He had a broad populist appeal, and he knew the political value of taking down the rich, especially in the middle of the depression. One of the first things he did upon taking office was hold a public auction in Toronto's Varsity Stadium, where he sold off all the government limousines. He fired the provincial film censor and ridiculed Toronto's clergy, who feared that the louche charms of the cinema would corrupt the province. "[These] pious so-called Christians," Hepburn said, "with souls that would just fit in a peanut shell, every once in a while have to shout from the house tops to justify their existence."

Hepburn appointed Eddie Odette, a friend and notoriously hard drinker, to oversee the liquor board. Within weeks, Odette issued 1,000 liquor licenses. The Liberal Prime Minister, Mackenzie King, a teetotaller, was appalled. Hepburn was against the unions, claiming communist infiltration and he created an anti-union security force, causing Mackenzie King to announce, "Hepburn has become a fascist leader."

Harold's estate pushed back against Hepburn, likely understanding that the premier's raid on large estates had more to do with politics than accounting. Hepburn wanted to be seen as Robin Hood, taking from the rich and giving to the poor. He wasn't able to get $800,000 out of Ritchie's heirs, but six months later, they settled for $350,000.

After Harold's death, the evolution from patent medicine to Big Pharma began to take shape. In 1924, a real estate mogul named Philip Hill gained control of Beecham for £2.8 million ($14 million Canadian), which had started as those pills made of ginger and soap sold by Harold. It had grown into a sizable company (370 million pills sold in 1913). One of the aspects of Beecham that attracted Hill was its profitability: its manufacturing costs were low, most of its employees were low-wage boys, and the advertising budget was three times the cost of manufacturing.

Hill essentially did what Harold had done—buy a successful drug company and expand into companies that sold beauty products. Four years after Berta sold Eno to the British trust company, Beecham bought controlling shares of Eno. Included in the sale was Thermogene and the three Harold F. Ritchie companies. What Hill wanted was the sales network that Harold had created. At a general meeting of the Beecham group in 1939, Hill told the assembled, "When your directors purchased the Eno business, one of their principal motives in doing so was to take advantage of the widespread export organization belonging to that company and to obtain the benefit of its specialized export experience covering a long period of time."

This view was echoed in an academic paper, "The Beecham Group in the World's Pharmaceutical Industry 1914-70," which stated, "Enos, of fruit salt fame, had an international network of selling agencies, on which Beecham's later built its post-1945 global expansion."

Hill kept the HFR + company management team in place, including Ruthven Hay as president and Glenn Robinson as sales manager. Hill used HFR + company to buy the County Perfumery Co., which made Brylcreem, the men's hair cream, and used the profits from that to help finance pharmaceutical research. It is highly unlikely that Harold would have sold Eno had he lived. He appeared to have been pursuing the same goal as Hill, only from a different direction. In one of Harold's last interviews, a journalist alluded to big projects in the works. "Even bigger things are contemplated," the journalist wrote. "It is known that at this very moment Mr. Ritchie is carrying on negotiations for other very large proprietaries, businesses, and there is every reason to believe that they will come to Canada." It isn't clear what these were, but they would likely have been patent medicines.

It would have been logical to team up with someone who had the research facilities for the next stage. Harold already had the sales network established, he had the manufacturing facilities, and he had expanded into beauty products as a way of financing research and development.

On October 1, 1960, HFR + company finally disappeared, officially changing its name to Beecham Canada. The Ritchie companies had been intertwined with Beecham, and Beecham then became interwoven with other budding pharmaceutical companies. In 1989, Beecham merged with SmithKline Beckman to become SmithKline Beecham. In 2000, it merged with GlaxoWellcome to become the pharmaceutical behemoth GlaxoSmithKline. Glaxo had had its start as the milk additive that "Builds Bonnie Babies," which Harold also sold. Like Beecham and others, it outgrew its early patent medicine beginnings into the much more lucrative world of drugs. The Harold F. Ritchie Company has been cited as one of the corporate ancestors of GlaxoSmithKline. On a GSK website, under the heading "Highlights in the History of GlaxoSmithKline Consumer

Healthcare Inc," the first two items are: "In 1907, Toronto-based Harold F. Ritchie & Company Ltd obtained the rights to distribute ENO Fruit Salts in Canada," and "In 1928, Mr. Ritchie acquired the UK-based companies JC Eno and Thermogene, forming a company called International Proprietaries Ltd."

Had Harold lived another twenty years, he would have likely been a key part of the pharmaceutical boom. Given that he was still expanding in 1932, it's difficult to believe he would have sold any of his companies. And since work was where most of his energy went, he certainly wasn't about to retire. A partnership with Beecham would have made a very large company poised to capitalize on the transition from patent medicine to pharmaceuticals. Harold's company would have been a more integral part of the merger that brought about GlaxoSmithKline. By 2019, GlaxoSmithKline was the eighth largest pharmaceutical company in the world, with $43.92 billion (US) in sales that year.

The interweaving of the various companies that eventually became the pharma giants were all connected to Harold in some capacity (Beecham even bought Bovril in 1980). The early research discoveries in the pharmaceutical world were relatively modest, and not entirely successful. What drove the industry, and continues to drive it, was sales and marketing. Harold had the largest sales force in the world, and one of the most sophisticated. And he had decades of experience selling and advertising patent medicines. Pharmaceuticals would have certainly been the "vaster career" that *Time* magazine hinted at in its obituary for Harold.

Berta had always been active in philanthropy and after Harold's death channelled her energies there. She kept up her volunteer work throughout her life and continued to travel. In 1935, she returned to London with Pauline and Antoinette, who were twenty and fourteen by then, as well as Kathleen and her husband, Tom Gilmour. In April 1936, she and Antoinette sailed to Bermuda for a vacation and stopped in New York on the way home. Two years later, she returned to Bermuda, this time in the company of Kay, Tom, and their three children. They were accompanied by two nannies, Mary Partridge and Violet Steer. Berta continued to travel, returning to London and Paris and Barbados, with various daughters and relatives. On one trip, the two nannies were Mary Partridge and Fern Peacock. The customs agent asked, "Are there any other feathered fowl in this party?"

Berta proved to be a great philanthropist, giving money and time to the Children's Aid Society, St. John Ambulance, and the Toronto General Hospital, among others. An award was created in her name, The St. John Ambulance's Alice Alberta Ritchie Award, presented to ambulance divisions for exceptional service. In 1941, she was district superintendent of the Toronto St. John Ambulance Brigade. Two years later, she was made a Dame of Grace of the Order of St. John.

And what of "Boy" Ritchie? It remains the great unsolved mystery of Harold's life. There is no mention of him in Harold's will. It seems odd, in that Harold made a point of including family and friends in his business, and all family members are included in the will. Boy would be Harold's only son, his first-born. If he was alive, and if Harold knew of his whereabouts, it seems likely he would have included him in the will. It's thought that he was raised on Manitoulin, although it's possible that the boy was given up for adoption off the island, and had no knowledge that Harold was his father. But had Harold wanted to seek him out, he certainly had the means to do so.

So, what are the possibilities? It's possible that Boy died. Mortality rates were relatively high back then. He would have been seventeen-years-old during the last year of the war; perhaps he enlisted. In the final years of the war, the government needed soldiers, and Boy wouldn't have been the first underage recruit to get overseas. He could be in a grave somewhere in France or Belgium. Or he could have lived a full life.

Whatever became of Harold's son, his daughters prospered. While Harold kept himself out of the society pages and at a distance from the Toronto establishment, his daughters were very much in the spotlight, their debuts into society, weddings, and honeymoon destinations reported in the local papers. And they all became an integral part of the Toronto establishment.

Kathleen's debutante ball in 1930 was a grand affair. The

Toronto Star reported it in detail, describing the dresses, the décor, and guests. "Just as mere words have ever been incapable of describing fairyland, so they completely fail to give an adequate conception of the splendour of the concert hall at the Royal York last night, when Mr. and Mrs. Harold Ritchie entertained for their debutante daughter, Miss Kathleen Ritchie." The event ended with breakfast at 4 a.m.

A year later, Kathleen married Tom Gilmour, a graduate of Upper Canada College who worked with McLeod Young Weir, and later for the Harold F. Ritchie Co. until the mid-thirties. Upon their engagement, Harold wrote to Tom, "I am very proud of you. You seem to have always felt about Kathleen as I did about her mother . . . I hope you will be as lucky as I have been. Come to me any time any place about anything."

Their wedding was covered by the local papers, featuring photographs of the bride and groom. The *Toronto Star* reported that the bridesmaids wore gowns of ivory satin, with roses and cornflowers. Tom went overseas during the Second World War, serving as Artillery Captain in the Canadian Army, before returning to civilian life in Toronto. Kathleen went on to become Lady Superintendent-in-Chief of the St. John Ambulance Brigade.

In September 1933, six months after Harold's death, Dorothy married Harold (Hal) Crang, a stockbroker who founded the firm J.H. Crang and Co. in 1929. Despite the inauspicious timing, his firm operated for many years. It was perhaps the most patrician small stock brokerage firm in Canadian history. Hal and Dorothy were married in the Bishop Strachan School chapel, where Dorothy and her sisters had gone to school. Hal had attended Upper Canada College, and served as a Major of the 7th Toronto Regiment Artillery during the Second World War. Known for his outstanding collection of antique silver, Hal was an honourary trustee of the Royal Ontario Museum. He enjoyed riding to the hounds with the Toronto and North York Hunt, and skeet shooting. In 1956, he set a skeet-shooting world record in England. He was also a fine photographer, taking a number of the photographs that appear in his book.

In April 1938, Pauline married Beverley Matthews, a lawyer with McCarthy & McCarthy (now McCarthy Tétrault). Like her sisters, Pauline was wed in the chapel at the Bishop Strachan School, with the reception at Hylands, as 40 Burton Road was known. Not long after the wedding, Bev went overseas with the 48th Highlanders of Canada. During the war, Pauline worked in a red cross canteen in London.

Bev Matthews left the army with the rank of Brigadier before returning to McCarthys, where he acted as managing partner and principal rainmaker over several decades. He served as chief fundraiser ("bagman") for the federal Progressive Conservative party under John Diefenbaker and Robert Stanfield. And he served on a number of major corporate boards, including Gulf

Oil in the United States, and the Toronto-Dominion Bank and TransCanada Pipelines in Canada.

Antoinette (known as Tony) had her debut at the Royal York Hotel in December 1938, with the *Toronto Star* describing her as "one of the season's most popular debutantes." Her married sisters were in attendance, their gowns described in detail. In June 1939, Tony married Charles Gundy, president and director of Wood Gundy & Co., which his father, Harry Gundy, had co-founded in 1905. The ceremony was in the chapel of Bishop Strachan School, with the reception held at Hylands.

Charles Gundy served with the Canadian Army in the Second World War, retiring with the rank of Major. He became one of Canada's best-known businessmen, sitting on a number of boards, including Abitibi Paper, Massey-Ferguson, and Canada Cement Lafarge. Under his leadership, Wood Gundy became Canada's leading investment firm.

Together, the Ritchie daughters probably received more press coverage than their father. And their husbands were pillars of the establishment that Harold had largely ignored during his lifetime. In his book *The Canadian Establishment,* Peter C. Newman wrote, "How an establishment organizes itself determines how a nation will pursue its objectives . . . Although their power is waning, they still possess the ability to compel obedience, to shape events and trends—political and cultural as well as economic . . ." Despite Harold's aloofness from the establishment, he loved Toronto, and his daughters and their husbands became part of the group that would define and shape the city's business community. Harold embraced his sons-in-law, but was more concerned with character than status. In a letter, he wrote, "I would much prefer to have our girls established in homes with husbands who are men of character and kindness & stability than men of mere position."

After Harold's death, Woodlands remained a refuge, a place for the family to gather in summer. Berta died on April 11, 1953. In 1955, a parcel of land was sold to Berta's youngest daughter, Tony Gundy. In 1961, the house and remaining property was sold to Berta's daughter, Pauline Matthews. It stayed in the Matthews family until 1998. In 2015, it was on the market for $16 million, although, by then, it included only fourteen of the original seventy acres.

Berta remained at 40 Burton Road until her death. Then Hal and Dorothy Crang moved in. Hal remained there after Dorothy died, and when Hal died, their son Rickey moved in. His daughters sold it after Rickey's death. It is now owned by Judy Bronfman.

Ruthven Hay died in 1951 at the age of seventy-six. He had been ill for a while. He is buried in Prospect Cemetery in Toronto. His wife, Mary Lavinia, died in 1968 and was buried beside her husband. Morland died in 1954 at the age of sixty and is buried in the Mountain View Cemetery in Little Current. He had remained there all his life, running the family store. In 1973, the

CARLOAD RITCHIE

Ritchie Bakery and Grocery Store burned to the ground. There is now a TD Bank on the site.

***

It was said of Harold, "Here is a real optimist in these suspicious times." That was an understatement. Harold was an eternal optimist and rarely seemed to be of his time; he always had one foot in the future. A journalist for *Canadian Magazine* described him as "restless, and during an interview he gives the impression of living and talking in the present but thinking a dozen jumps ahead of the game." He changed the way travelling salesmen operated, and then changed sales, creating a multi-national, professional, sophisticated organization that replaced the travelling salesman. He was unfazed by the First World War, the Spanish Flu or the depression. Bullets flew, economies crashed, companies went bankrupt, and through it all of Harold's world continued to expand. In South America, he shrugged off revolutions and juntas and chaos. All of this would pass, and when it did, people would still need coffee and tea and beans and butter and comfort from life's ravages.

Perhaps it was fitting that most of what the public knew about Harold came from his obituaries. They appeared in papers around the world, telling the same story: a boy grows up in the middle of nowhere and starts a global empire.

CARLOAD'S LEGACY

Harold kept much from his Manitoulin childhood. It is clear that those people and that place remained in his heart. The Great Spirit, the Kiche Manitou that created Manitoulin Island and the rest of the universe, bestowed upon man the power to dream. Few dreamed as big as Harold F. Ritchie.

Sources

CHAPTER ONE

Irish immigration figures come from the History Channel website.

P. 7: the Indigenous history is taken from Shelley J. Pearen's book *Exploring Manitoulin*, and from the Treaty Research Report by Robert J. Surtees.

P. 9: the land sales figures are from *Reflections of Howland, Little Current, and Vicinity*. Other Manitoulin material is from *Mer Douce, Vol I: The Story of Ontario*, *The Expositor*, and interviews with local historian Sandy McGillivray.

P. 21: The immigration pamphlet information is from *Canada: A People's History, Volume II*, by Don Gillmor.

P. 22: Harold's quotes are taken from an interview with the *Toronto Telegram*.

Also, Boyter information is from *Murders and Mysteries of the Manitoulin District*, Willis John McQuarrie.

CARLOAD RITCHIE

CHAPTER TWO

P. 25: Background on Berta from Ancestry.ca and family, and from Mary Gundy.

P. 29: South African material is from *A Canadian Girl in South Africa*, E. Maud Graham.

P. 31: Harold's rescue of girl: *Ottawa Citizen*, July 24, 1903.

CHAPTER THREE

P. 42: Harold and Forest Hill councillors, *Globe* January 26/1925.

P. 45: NCR information, *Birth of a Salesman*, Walter Friedman.

P. 47: Harold's sales convention, *Globe* January 5, 1921.

P. 49: Harold's quotes are from *Toronto Telegram* interview.

Also, shipping records from Mary Gundy; First World War material from *Legion Magazine*.

CHAPTER FOUR

P. 50: Harold's quote from the *Toronto Telegram* interview.

P. 60: Quotes from Eno celebration are from official minutes of Diamond Jubilee evening, July 6, 1928.

Also, patent medicine material from Pharmaforum, September 1, 2020; *Torontoist*, May 31, 2011; Illinois State University archives, Chemical & Engineering News.

SOURCES

CHAPTER FIVE

P. 68: Pompeian material, *Globe*, May 3, 1930.

P. 73: South America trip material is from *Globe*, August 13, 1932, and *Victoria Times Colonist* and *The Windsor Star*, November 26, 1932.

P. 79: Harold's quotes, *Globe*, January 19, 1933.

CHAPTER SIX

P. 81: History of Woodlands is courtesy of the Porter family.

Also, Arthur Peuchen material from the *Canadian Encyclopedia* and the *Encyclopedia Titanica*. Sale price of $16 million from *Barrie Today*.

CHAPTER SEVEN

P. 88: Family material from family members, Ancestry.ca.

P. 89: *Globe and Mail* headline is from *Globe*, May 8, 1935.

P. 89: Mitchell Hepburn material from *Canada: A People's History, Vol II*, Don Gillmor.

P. 89: Harold's estate, *Globe*, May 13, 1933.

P. 94-98: Material from the family.

P. 97: *Canadian Magazine*, June 1930.

Acknowledgments

THANK YOU TO Toni Allen, Susan Dutton, Biff Matthews, Geoff Matthews, and especially the indefatigable Mary Gundy for their help and research. Thanks to Mark and Cathy Porter (current owners of Woodlands) for the wonderful tour of their property, and to Sandy McGillivray for his time and knowledge.